Sufi Poems

OTHER BOOKS BY MARTIN LINGS
AVAILABLE FROM THE ISLAMIC TEXTS SOCIETY

Muhammad: His Life
Based on the Earliest Sources

The Book of Certainty: the Sufi Doctrine of
Faith, Vision and Gnosis

A Sufi Saint of the Twentieth Century:
Shaikh Aḥmad al-ʿAlawī

What is Sufism?

The Holy Qur'ān:
Translations of Selected Verses
(in preparation)

SUFI POEMS

A Mediaeval Anthology

Arabic and English edition
compiled and translated by
Martin Lings

THE ISLAMIC TEXTS SOCIETY

First published in 2004 by
The Islamic Texts Society
Miller's House
Kings Mill Lane
Great Shelford
Cambridge CB22 5EN, U.K.

Reprint 2006, 2012

Set with ArabTEX and pdfTEX
in Latin Modern and Naskh types.
The publishers wish to thank
Prof. Klaus Lagally (Stuttgart) for his generous help.

British Library Cataloguing-in-Publication Data.
A catalogue record for this book is
available from the British Library.

ISBN 978 1903682 18 0 cloth
ISBN 978 1903682 17 3 paper

The Islamic Texts Society is distributed in North America by:

Independent Publishers Group
814 North Franklin Street, Chicago, IL 60610, USA
www.ipgbook.com

Contents

Preface vii

1 Rābiʿah al-ʿAdawiyyah 1

2 Dhu'n-Nūn al-Miṣrī 7

3 Sahl at-Tustarī 13

4 Abū Ḥusayn an-Nūrī 16

5 Sumnūn al-Muḥibb 21

6 Manṣūr al-Ḥallāj 26

7 Abū Bakr ash-Shiblī 41

8 Abū'l-ʿAbbās as-Sayyārī 47

9 ʿAbd al-ʿAzīz at-Tūnisī 51

10 Abū Ḥāmid al-Ghazālī 55

11 Muḥyī'd-Dīn Ibn ʿArabī 59

12 ʿUmar Ibn al-Fāriḍ 66

13 Abū'l-Ḥasan ash-Shushtarī 84

Conclusion 91

Notes 93

Bibliography 102

Preface

Thou art That—This Hindu expression of what is often called the Supreme Identity has necessarily its equivalent in all other religions. In Islam, of which Sufism is the innermost aspect, the truth in question is expressed by the Qur'ān in the words: 'We [God] are nearer to him [man] than his jugular vein;' and as we shall see, one of the poems contained in this volume opens with the words:

> I saw my Lord with the eye of the Heart.
> I said: 'Who art Thou?' He answered: 'Thou.'

Ḥallāj, the author of these lines, defines elsewhere this identity as an 'intermittent identification'; and the great Algerian Master, Shaykh Aḥmad al-ʿAlawī, about whom I wrote my book *A Sufi Saint of the Twentieth Century*, fully confirms this intermittence.[1] He speaks of God as 'taking one of His slaves to Himself and bringing him into His Presence where sometimes He reveals Himself to him and sometimes withdraws from him.' The word 'where' is all-important.

These absences within the framework of Presence can be seen as inevitable in the light of the truth that the existence of a holy man herebelow is always providential. The Oneness of Union, which effaces all but Itself, will therefore providentially release Its hold on the human nature of a Saint so that he may fulfil his earthly function as a spiritual guide for some, and as an example for all who may encounter him.

This same inevitability is also clearly to be seen from another standpoint. To speak of a holy man or woman is to

---

[1] *A Sufi Saint of the Twentieth Century: Shaykh Aḥmad al-ʿAlawī, his Spiritual Heritage and Legacy*, Cambridge, Islamic Texts Society, 1993, p. 165.

speak of one who has at least regained the primordial state, that is, the human perfection which man, as yet unfallen, possessed in the Earthly Paradise; and that perfection, like the Garden of Eden itself, is nothing other than a reflection of what lies above it in the Next World, in the Celestial Paradises and in the Blessed Spirits who abide in them. Therefore, since the Qur'ān promises, for every faithful soul, two Paradises, the need for that duality cannot fail to be already apparent in the Saint herebelow, as we have already seen it to be, that is, in the regular alternation of his spirituality from one state to another.

The Qur'ān mentions two pairs of Paradises, which need not necessarily be taken literally, in a limitative sense, but it is clearly the highest pair which may be said to belong to all who have attained to the supreme degree of Sainthood. According to a Sufi commentary[2] this pair consists of the Paradise of the Spirit and the Paradise of the Essence. The communion of the Saints takes place in the Paradise of the Spirit which is characterised, as far as its fruit is concerned, by the date because, according to the commentary, 'the kernel of the individuality still remains', whereas the Paradise of the Essence is characterised by the pomegranate which has no kernel. This is the Paradise of Union, in which every individuality is extinguished. But since all the Paradises are within the aura of the Divine Essence there can be no sense of deprivation when Union gives way to a certain differentiation of Spirits. Otherwise expressed, the marvellous presences which are to be encountered are too eloquently manifestations of the Divine Essence Itself to give rise to anything but joyous wonderment. But herebelow Saints are no longer in the Paradise of Eden, and as things are and have been throughout historic times, the sense of separation from God and the return to the intrusive imperfections of this lower world can be overwhelming, despite the certitude of the Saint that the state of Union cannot be lost and that every apparent absence is within the framework of Presence. The soul spontaneously seeks a means of relief, and the chief means, needless to say, is prayer. Another means of relief, not altogether unconnected with prayer, is to give birth to a poem.

[2]See Abū Bakr Sirāj ad-Dīn, *The Book of Certainty*, Cambridge, Islamic Texts Society, 1992, p. IX, note 1.

It is therefore not surprising that some of the poems in this volume should be plaintive; but its preface has partly been written to make it clear that this apparent distress is by no means necessarily a sign that the poet in question had not yet attained to the supreme spiritual state.

The project of putting together this small volume goes back as far as the mid-seventies. A year or two later, before I had begun to work on it, I was asked by the late Professor Sergeant to write the chapter on Sufi poetry—it was finally entitled 'Mystical Poetry'—for Volume 2 of *The New Cambridge History of Arabic Literature.*[3] I agreed to do so on the condition, to which he assented, that I should retain the copyright, not for the chapter as a whole but for the translations of the poems quoted in the chapter, and I told him of my intention of compiling an anthology of mediæval Sufi poetry.

This does not mean that the poems contained in the chapter are exactly the same as those which follow. For the chapter I was limited to a certain number of words so that, by way of example, it contains only the beginning and the end of Ibn al-Fāriḍ's *Wine-Song*, whereas here we have the whole poem, in addition to other shorter poems that likewise had to be left out of the chapter. Nonetheless, for what it contains apart from quotations, I think that the chapter might be of considerable interest to any interested reader of this anthology.

In this present volume, the poems of each poet are grouped together; and the order of the groups, but not that of the poems within each group, is chronological as far as possible.

Martin Lings

[3] J. Ashtiany (ed.), *ʿAbbasid Belles-Lettres*, Cambridge, Cambridge University Press, 1990.

1

Rābiʿah al-ʿAdawiyyah of Basrah

(d. 185 AH/801 AD)

Having been born about 100 years after the establishment of Islam, she cannot be said to have experienced anything of the harmonious unity which had characterised the first decades of the new religion. Her whole life was set in a time of rapidly increasing worldliness. As I have said elsewhere[1]: 'It was her vocation —we might almost say mission, for such was her greatness— to incarnate at the highest level, that is, in the domain of the Spirit, the putting of first things first—God before Paradise, the Absolute before the relative. It was in this sense that she would quote *al-jār thumma 'd-dār* (the neighbour, then the house), the Arab version of the world-wide maxim that in choosing a house, it is more important to see who is going to be your neighbour than what the house itself is like.' Rābiʿah is especially remembered for her reply to a man who came to seek her spiritual advice on the basis of the fact, so he maintained, that he had not sinned for twenty years: 'Alas my son, thine existence is a sin wherewith no other sin can be compared.'[2]

1

Two loves I give Thee, love that yearns,
And love because Thy due is love.
My yearning my remembrance turns
To Thee, nor lets it from Thee rove.
Thou hast Thy due whene'er it please Thee
To lift the veils for me to see Thee.
Praise is not mine in this, nor yet
In that, but Thine in this and that.[3]

2

Brethren, my rest is in my solitude,
And my Beloved is ever in my presence.
Nothing for me will do but love of Him;
By love of Him I am tested in this world.
Whereso I be I contemplate His beauty;
He is my prayer-niche; He mine orient is.
Died I of love and found not His acceptance,
Of mankind I most wretched, woe were me!
Heart's mediciner, Thou All of longing, grant
Union with Thee; 'twill cure me to the depth.
O Thou, ever my joy, my life, from Thee
Is mine existence and mine ecstasy.
From all creation I have turned away
For union with Thee—mine utmost end.[4]

١

أُحِبُّكَ حُبَّيْنِ حُبَّ الهَوَى   وحُبّاً لأنَّكَ أهْلٌ لِذَاكا
فَأمّا الّذي هوَ حُبُّ الهَوىَ   فَشُغْلي بِذِكرِكَ عَمَّنْ سِوَاكا
وأمّا الّذي أَنْتَ أهْلٌ لَهُ   فَكَشْفُكَ لِلْحُجْبِ حتّى أرَاكا
فَلاَ الحَمْدُ في ذَا ولاَ ذَاكَ لِي   وَلَكِنْ لَكَ الحَمْدُ فِي ذَا وذَاكَا

٢

رَاحتي يَا إخْوَتِي في خَلْوَتِي   وحَبِيبِي دَائِمًا فِي حَضْرَتِي
لَمْ أجِدْ لي عَنْ هَوَاهُ عِوَضاً   وهَوَاهُ فِي البَرَايَا مِحْنَتِي
حَيْثُما كُنْتُ أُشَاهِدُ حُسْنَهُ   فَهُوَ مِحْرابِي إِلَيْهِ قِبْلَتِي
إنْ أَمُتْ وَجْداً وما ثَمَّ رِضَا   وَاعَنَائِي فِي الوَرَى واشِقْوَتِي
يَا طَبِيبَ القَلْبِ يَاكُلَّ المُنَى   جُدْ بِوَصْلٍ مِنكَ يَشْفِي مُهْجَتِي
يَا سُرُورِي وحَيَاتِي دَائِماً   نَشْأَتِي مِنْكَ وأيْضًا نَشْوَتِي
قَدْ هَجَرْتُ الخَلْقَ جَمْعاً أرْتَجِي   مِنكَ وَصْلاً فهوَ أقْصَى مُنْيَتِي

3

Thy prayer is a light and thy worship a rest,
But wilfully thy sleep these devotions outbalanceth.
Thy life, didst but know it, is a chance not to be missed,
And brief is its respite, ever-dwindling, then it perisheth.[5]

4

Thou me my spirit through and through[6]
Hast penetrated: even so
A thorough friend must thorough be.
So, when I speak, I speak of Thee;
When silent, then I long for Thee.[7]

٣

صَلاَتُكَ نُورٌ والعِبَادُ رُقُودُ
ونَوْمُكَ ضِدٌ للصَلاَةِ عَنِيدُ
وعُمْرُكَ غُنْمٌ إنْ عَقَلْتَ ومَهْلُهُ
يَسِيرُ وَيَفْنَى دَائِماً ويَبِيدُ

٤

قَدْ تَخَلَّلْتَ مَسْلَكَ الرُّوحِ مِنِّي
ولِذَا سُمِّيَ الخَلِيلُ خَلِيلاَ
فَإذَا مَا نَطَقْتُ كُنْتَ حَدِيثِي
وإذَا مَا سَكَتُّ كُنْتَ الغَلِيلاَ

2

Dhu'n-Nūn Thawbān al-Miṣrī of Ikhmīm in Upper Egypt

(d. 246 AH/861 AD)

His father was a Nubian and presumably a slave, since Dhu'n-Nūn himself was said to be a freedman. In his maturity, he came to be known throughout the Near East as 'the head of the Sufis'. He left no treatises on Sufism, but thanks to many devoted disciples a wealth of treasures has survived from his recorded teachings on fundamental aspects of Sufi doctrine and method. Many of his own personal prayers have also come down to us, together with some poems.

Like some other Sufis, he fearlessly maintained the doctrinal tenets of Orthodox Islam, in particular as regards the uncreatedness of the Qur'ān, which brought him into conflict with the somewhat heretical ruling party. He was even arrested, at one time towards the end of his life, and sent to prison in Baghdad, nor did the Sufis of that city fail to take advantage of his presence there. But it was not long before he was set free by order of the Caliph, and he returned to Egypt. He spent his last years on the outskirts of Cairo in Giza, and it is there that he died and is buried.

5

I die, but my passion for Thee dieth not.
Unfulfilled are my longings to drink deep Thy love.
My desires are the essence of all desire; Thou art they;
And Thou art riches, all riches, for me in my beggary.
Thou art the goal of my quest, the full scope of my wish,
The theme of my plaint, the hidden depths of my consciousness.
Burdened through Thee is my heart with what I tell not,
Howso long be my ailing for Thee and my constraint.
And from Thee, in my breast is what clearly Thou seest,
Though its clarity is not clear unto kinsman or neighbour;
And within me a spreading sickness hath weakened my frame,
And my secret confiding unto Thee is poured forth.
Art Thou not guide to lost travellers in bewilderment,
And saviour from the brink of the crumbling precipice?
Whom Thou guidest, Thou lightest their way, when themselves
They have not one tenth of one tenth of the light.
Vouchsafe me then favour, that in its nearness I may live.
Help me with ease from Thee, my hardship to repel.[8]

٥

أموتُ وَما ماتَتْ إلَيكَ صَبابَتِي
ولا قُضِيَتْ مِنْ صِدْقِ حُبّكَ أوْطارِي
مُنايَ المُنَى كُلُّ المُنَى أنْتَ لِي مُنىً
وأنْتَ الغِنَى كُلُّ الغِنَى عِنْدَ افْتِقارِي
وأنْتَ مَدَى سُؤلِي وغَايَةُ رَغْبَتِي
ومَوْضِعُ آمَالِي ومَكْنُونُ أضْمَارِي
تحَمَّلَ قَلْبي فِيكَ مَا لاَ أبُثُّهُ
وَإنْ طالَ سُقْمِي فِيك أوْ طالَ إضْرارِي
وبَيْنَ ضُلُوعِي مِنْكَ مَا لَكَ قَدْ بَدَا
وَلَمْ يَبْدُ بادِيهِ لأهْلٍ ولاَ جَارِ
وَبِي مِنْكَ فِي ألأحْشَاءِ دَاءٌ مُخامِرٌ
فَقَدْ هَدَّ مِنِي الرّكْنَ وانْبَثَّ إسْرَارِي
ألَسْتَ دَلِيلَ الرَكْبِ إنْ هُمْ تحَيَّرُوا
ومُنْقِذَ من أشْفى عَلَى جُرُفٍ هَارِي
أنَرْتَ الهُدَى لِلمُهْتَدِينَ وَلَمْ يَكُنْ
مِنَ النُّورِ فِي أيْدِيهِمُ عُشْرُ مِعْشَارِ
فَنَلْنِي بِعَفْوٍ مِنْكَ أَحْيَا بِقُرْبِهِ
أغِثْنِي بِيُسْرٍ مِنْكَ يَطْرُدُ إعْسَارِي

6

The haunt of the hearts of the gnostics is a mead
Celestial—beyond it are the veils of the Lord,
His nearness their sole boundary from the world of the Secret—
Melt they would with love if their moment had come.
For their thirst is a cup purely filled from His love,
And the cool of a breeze beyond words to describe.
Hearts near the Throne-Lord—they had sought to be near—
With what blessings the King in their nearness hath graced
[them!
Pleased with them, He hath pleased them unto ultimate pleasure:
The Beloved's welcome is the abode wherein they dwell,
Most penetrant their resolve; by it they have travelled,
By it their thoughts pierce to what is hidden by the Veils.
Their secret ever goeth between the Beloved and themselves,
From other than nearness by nearness made safe.[9]

٦

مَجَالُ قُلُوبِ العَارِفِينَ بِرَوْضَةٍ
سَمَاوِيَةٍ مِنْ دُونِهَا حُجُبُ الرَّبِّ
تَكَنَّفَهَا مِنْ عَالَمِ السِّرِّ قُرْبُهُ
فَلَوْ قَدَّرَ الآجَالَ ذَابَتْ مِنَ الحُبِّ
وأروى صَداها كأسُ صِرْفٍ بِحُبِّهِ
وبَرْدُ نَسِيمٍ جَلَّ عَنْ مُنْتَهى الخَطْبِ
فَيَا لِقُلُوبٍ قُرِّبَتْ فَتَقَرَّبَتْ
لِذَا الْعَرْشِ مِمّا زُيِّنَ المَلِكُ بِالقُرْبِ
رَضِيَها فأَرْضَاهَا فَحَازَتْ مَدَى الرِّضَى
وحَلَّتْ مِنَ المَحبوبِ بِالْمَنْزِلِ الرَّحْبِ
لَهَا مِنْ لَطِيفِ العَزْمِ عَزْمٌ سَرَتْ بِهِ
وتَهْتِكُ بالأَفْكَارِ مَا داخِلَ الحُجُبِ
سَرَى سِرُّهَا بَيْنَ الحَبِيبِ وَبَيْنِهَا
فأَضْحَى مَصُوناً عَنْ سِوَى القُرْبِ فِي القُرْبِ

3

Sahl ibn ʿAbd Allāh at-Tustarī of Basra

(d. 283 AH/896 AD)

Dhu'n-Nūn's younger contemporary, Tustarī, is better known for his prose works, in particular for one of the first mystical commentaries on the Qur'ān. Like his predecessor he was one of the greatest of the early Sufis, and his generally recognized authority brought him many disciples.

7

The gnostics' hearts with eyes are blest
That see what other see-ers see not;
And tongues whose discourse is of secrets
Beyond the recording angels' ken,[10]
And wings that all unfeathered fly
To His dominion, Lord of the Worlds.
We have inherited the draught,
Sciences of hidden secret,
Rarer than all lore of old.
Their samples speak for them as signs[11]
And nullify impostors' claims.[12]

٧

قُلُوبُ العَارِفِينَ لَهَا عُيُونٌ   تَرَى مَا لاَ يَرَاهُ النَّاظِرِينَا
وأَلْسِنَةٌ بِأَسْرارٍ تُنَاجِي   تَغِيبُ عَنِ الْكِرَامِ الْكَاتِبِينَا
وأَجْنِحَةٌ تَطِيرُ بِغَيْرِ رِيشٍ   إِلَى مَلَكُوتِ رَبِّ العَالَمِينَا
فَأَوْرَثَنَا الشَّرَابُ عُلُومَ غَيْبٍ   تَشِفُّ عَلَى عُلُومِ الأَقْدَمِينَا
شَوَاهِدُهَا عَلَيْهَا نَاطِقَاتٌ   وتُبْطِلُ كُلَّ دَعْوَى المُدَّعِينَا

4

Abū Ḥusayn Aḥmad ibn Muḥammad an-Nūrī of Baghdad

(d. 295 AH/907 AD)

Towards the end of the third century of Islam, there were many remarkable spiritual men in Baghdad who are often spoken of collectively as the Baghdad School of Sufis. One of those who is most often quoted by them and who was in fact a generation older than most of them, is Sarī as-Saqaṭī (d. 253 AH/867 AD); but though I have no poems of his to offer my readers,[13] it is to him that we owe the survival of the following lines, two in the original, by an un-named Sufi.

> Sarī as-Saqaṭī said: 'I was with an Ethiopian[14] in the wilderness, and I saw that whenever he invoked Allāh his colour changed and he became whiter. So I said to him: "Marvellous to relate, whenever thou invokest Allāh thine expression changeth and thine appearance is altered." Then he said: "O my brother, as to thee thyself, shouldst thou invoke Allāh according to His due of invocation, thine expression would change and thine appearance would be altered." Then he recited:

We were invoking, nor ever forgot, but lo!
The zephyr of Nearness[15] breathed, Its radiance shone,
And I, thereby extinct from me, in Him
As His subsisted, for Reality
Proclaimeth Him, to none but Him refereth.'[16]

ذَكَرْنَا وَما كُنَّا لِنَنْسى فَنَذْكُرُ   وَلَكِنْ نَسِيمُ الْقُرْبِ يَبْدُو فَيَبْهَرُ
فَأَفْنى بِهِ عَنّى وَأَبْقى بِهِ لَهُ   إِذْ الحَقُّ عَنْهُ مُخْبِرٌ وَمُعَبِّرُ

The best known of Sarī's disciples is his nephew and successor, Abu'l-Qāsim al-Junayd. In fact Sufism looks back to him as one of its supreme authorities, and for the sake of this volume as a whole, and in particular as we shall see, for the sake of Nūrī, it will not be out of place to dwell briefly here on this illustrious representative of what lies at the root of the poems here given. It is to Junayd that we owe the following precious definition: 'Sufism is that God should make thee die away from thyself and live in Him.' Also relevant to this anthology is the following statement by Junayd about the grace of intimacy (*uns*) with God. 'I heard Sarī say: "The slave may reach a point wherein if his face were struck with a sword he would not notice it," and there was something in my heart which assented to this even before the time came when I saw clearly that it was as he had said.'[17]

To come now, at long last, to Nūrī himself, who was likewise a disciple of Sarī, he seems to have been Junayd's most intimate friend. Each of them had, in due course, his own disciples. Junayd died about three years after Nūrī and is said to have asked, on his deathbed, to be buried beside Nūrī, but we may suppose that the Saqaṭī family had 'better' plans, since the tomb of Junayd is in fact in a spacious shrine which contains only one other tomb, that of his uncle Sarī.

The name an-Nūrī is not a family name but an honorific title, 'man of light', bestowed on him perhaps by Junayd who is said to have often stressed Nūrī's penetration into the souls of his disciples. It was also said that when he spoke in a dark room, the room would grow lighter, as if lit by the light of truth.

8

Be unto me as Thou wast when I was not,
O Thou for whom I am beset by calamity and sorrow![18]

9

From time I'm veiled; my veil is my concern for Him,
My wonder at His Infinite worth transcending mine.
That I am absent from its grasp time see-eth not,
And I perceive not time's events, how they flow on,
Since I am all attendance to fulfil His due,
Nor care I, all my life long, for the hand of time.[19]

10

I would, so overflowing is my love for Him,
Remember Him perpetually, yet my remembrance—
Wondrous to tell—is vanished into ecstasy,
And wonder upon wonder, even ecstasy,
With memory's self, in nearness-farness vanished is.[20]

٨

كُنْ لِي كَمَا كُنْتَ لِي فِي حِينِ لَمْ أَكُنْ
يَا مَنْ بِهِ صِرْتُ بَيْنَ الرُّزْءِ والحَزَنْ

٩

تَسَتَّرْتُ عَنْ دَهْرِي بِسِتْرِ هُمُومِهِ
مُحَيَّرَةً فِي قَدْرِ مَنْ جَلَّ عَنْ قَدْرِي
فَلاَ الدَّهْرُ يَدْرِي أَنَّنِي عَنْهُ غَائِبٌ
وَلاَ أَنَا أَدْرِي بِالخُطُوبِ إِذَا تَجْرِي
إِذَا كَانَ كُلِّي قَائِماً بِوَفَائِهِ
فَلَسْتُ أُبَالِي مَا حَيِيتُ يَدَ الدَّهْرِ

١٠

أُرِيدُ دَوَامَ الذِّكْرِ مِنْ فَرْطِ حُبِّهِ
فَيَا عَجَباً مِنْ غَيْبَةِ الذِّكْرِ فِي الوَجْدِ
وَأَعْجَبُ مِنْهُ غَيْبَةُ الوَجْدِ تَارَةً
وَغَيْبَةُ عَيْنِ الذِّكْرِ فِي القُرْبِ وَالبُعْدِ

5

Abū'l-Ḥasan Sumnūn ibn Ḥamzah al-Baṣrī of Baghdad

(d. 303 AH/915 AD)

Sumnūn had known Sarī as-Saqaṭī and, like Nūrī, he was a close friend of Junayd. Also like Nūrī he was given a title. In his case it was *al-Muḥibb*, the Lover; but it would be a grave mistake to suppose that his way was fundamentally unlike that of his associates. The same applies to the title *Sulṭān al-ʿĀshiqīn*, the Sultan of the Yearners, given to ʿUmar ibn al-Fāriḍ who was, as we shall see, profoundly intellectual. In both cases it was a question of love within the framework of gnosis, which is the norm of Sufism; and we will open our selection of Sumnūn's poems with a couplet which is a masterly expression of that norm.

11

A witness's existence is extinguished by That which he witnesseth.
It extinguisheth existence and maketh it meaningless.
Thou hast thrown me to swim in the Ocean of Thy Holiness,
Where inexistent without trace I desire Thee from within Thee.[21]

12

Thou'rt the Beloved—no doubt is in my breast.
My soul, were it to lose Thee, would not live.
Thou who hast made me thirst so longingly
For union which Thou hast power to give,
Were there for me in Thee a place of rest,
If 'Oh, my thirst, my thirst!' I cried to Thee.[22]

13

If ever once mine eye a vigil kept,
For other than Thyself, or if it wept,
Be it ne'er given the gift it was inspired
To long for, and so longingly desired!
If e'er it did deliberately gaze
On other than Thyself, may it ne'er graze
Upon the Meadows of Felicity,
Thy Countenance! May its sight darkened be.[23]

١١

أفْنَى الوُجودَ بِشاهِدٍ مَشْهُودُهُ

يُفْنِي الوجودَ وكُلَّ مَعْنىً يَحْضُرُ

وطَرَحْتَنِي في بَحْرِ قُدْسِكَ سابِحاً

أبْغِيكَ مِنْكَ بِلا وُجودٍ يَظْهَرُ

١٢

أَنْتَ الحَبِيبُ الّذِي لاَ شَكَّ فِي خَلَدِي

مِنْهُ فَإِنْ فَقَدَتْكَ النَّفْسُ لَمْ تَعِشِ

يَا مُعْطِشي بِوِصالٍ أَنْتَ واهِبُهُ

هَلْ فِيكَ لِي راحَةٌ إِنْ صِحْتُ واعَطَشِي

١٣

مَتَى سَهِرَتْ عَيْنِي لِغَيْرِكَ أَوْ بَكَتْ

فَلاَ أُعْطِيَتْ ما مُنِيّتْ وَتَمَنَّتِ

وإِنْ أَضْمَرَتْ يَوْماً سِوَاكَ فَلاَ رَعَتْ

رِيَاضَ المُنَى مِنْ وَجْنَتَيْكَ وجُنَّتِ

14

Empty I was within me ere Thy love I found,
Idly on men and things I thought, oft merry-making,
But when Thy love summoned my heart, it did respond,
Nor can I see it ever now Thy court forsaking.
May I be smitten with severance from Thee if I lie.
If in this world I ever joy in aught but Thee,
If any thing in any land ever to me
Seem beautiful, if Thou art absent from mine eye!
So take me to Thee, if Thou wilt, or say me no,
Whiche'er it be, for none but Thee my heart will do.[24]

15

With yearning at each dawn and dusk I long,
And when at night love calls I answer her.
More our days vanish, more my love grows strong,
Even as if love's time unvanishing were.[25]

١٤

وكَانَ فُؤادِي خَالِياً قَبْلَ حُبِّكُمْ
وكَانَ بِذِكْرِ الخَلْقِ يَلْهُو وَيَمْـزَحُ
فَلَمّا دَعَا قَلْبِي هَـوَاكَ أَجَابَهُ
فَلَسْتُ أَرَاهُ عَنْ فِنَائِكَ يَبْرَحُ
رُمِيتُ بِبَيْنٍ مِنْكَ إِنْ كُنْتُ كاذِباً
وإِنْ كُنْتُ فِي الدُّنْيا بِغَيْرِكَ أَفْرَحُ
وإِنْ كَانَ شَيْءٌ في البِلاَدِ بأَسْرِهَا
إِذَا غِبْتَ عَنْ عَيْني بِعَيْني يَمْلُحُ
فإِنْ شِئْتَ واصِلْني وإِنْ شِئْتَ لاتَصِلْ
فَلَسْتُ أَرَى قَلْبِي لِغَيْرِكَ يَصْلُحُ

١٥

أَحِنُّ بأَطْرافِ النَّهارِ صَبابَةً   وفي اللّيْلِ يدعُوني الهَوَى فَأُجِيبُ
وأَيامُنا تَفْنَى وشَـوْقِي زائِدٌ   كَأَنَّ زَمانَ الشَّوْقِ لَيْسَ يَغِيبُ

6

Al-Ḥusayn ibn Manṣūr al-Ḥallāj of Baghdad

(d. 309 AH/922 AD)

Ḥallāj is said to have been, as a young man, the disciple of Tustarī and then of Junayd, whose favourite disciple, Abū Bakr ash-Shiblī, was a friend of Ḥallāj and, as we shall soon see, his fellow poet. Both these disciples were temperamentally a contrast to their master, who felt that they were lacking in sobriety and reticence, far too ready to utter profound spiritual truths in the presence of those who could not possibly understand them. But whereas Shiblī's discipleship lasted until the death of Junayd, whose successor he is generally considered to have been, Ḥallāj does not appear to have been the disciple of any master during the last part of his life. His death at the age of sixty-five was the result of his being accused of heresy for having said: 'I am the Truth.' These words occur in one of his poems, but it is not known whether the accusation resulted from the poem or from one of his spontaneous ejaculations. However that may be, after a trial that lasted for seven months, he was found guilty and put to death, in 309 AH/922 AD, with monstrous cruelty. But the verdict against him, which was final for his life on earth, has proved to be anything but final in other respects. His case has been re-tried by every succeeding generation of Muslims down to the present day, nor did it take long for the verdict 'no man has the right to speak these words' to be annulled in favour of the appeal 'man was not in this case the speaker.' The words in question have in fact come to be part of the overwhelming evidence that Ḥallāj must be given a place among the greatest Saints recorded by history; and needless to say, this opinion has been shared by a gradually increasing number of mystics from other religions, as well as those who, without practising mysticism, have made a serious study of it.[26] But let us allow the poems to speak for themselves.

16

To thee a long-hid secret is revealed,
A day-break dawns from the night's dark, from thee;
The heart's veil o'er its secret mystery
Art thou, nor, but for thee, had it been sealed.[27]

17

One with Thee make me, O my One, through Oneness
Faithed in sincerity no path can reach.
I am the Truth, and Truth, for Truth, is Truth,
Robed in Its Essence, thus beyond separation.
Lo, they are manifest, the brightnesses
That from Thy dawning Presence scintillate,
Each gleam a brilliance like the lightning flash.[28]

18

Is it I or Thou? These twain! Two gods!
Far be it, far be it from me to affirm two!
Selfhood is Thine in my nothingness forever:
Mine all, over all, casts illusion twofold:
For where is Thine Essence, where from me, for me to see,
When mine hath no where, as already is plain?
And Thy Countenance, where with my two sights may I seek it,
In the seeing of my heart, or the seeing of mine eye?
Twixt Thee and me an 'I am' is, o'ercrowding me:
Take, by Thine own 'I am', mine from between us.[29]

19

I saw my Lord with the eye of the heart.
I said: 'Who art thou?' He answered: 'Thou.'
Thus where no where hath, as from Thee,
Nor is there, as to Thee, a where.
Thou giv'st imagining no image
For it to imagine where Thou art.
He art Thou who hath filled all where—
Beyond where too. Where art Thou then?[30]

١٦

بَدَا لَكَ سِرٌّ طَالَ عَنْكَ اكْتِتَامُهُ   ولاَحَ صَبَاحٌ كُنْتَ أنْتَ ظَلاَمَهُ
وأنْتَ حِجَابُ القَلْبِ عَنْ سِرِّ غَيْبِهِ   وَلوْلاَكَ لَمْ يُطْبَعْ عَلَيْهِ خِتَامُهُ

١٧

وَحِّدْنِي وَاحِدِي بِتَوْحِيدِ صِدْقٍ   ما إلَيْهِ مِنَ المَسَالِكِ طُرُقُ
أنَا الحَقُّ والحَقُّ لِلْحَقِّ حَقٌّ   لاَبِسٌ ذاتَهُ فَمَا ثَمَّ فَرْقُ
قَدْ تَجَلَّتْ طَوالِعٌ زاهِرَاتٌ   يَتَشَعْشَعْنَ فِي لَوَامِعِ بَرْقِ

١٨

آهٍ أنَا أمْ أنْتَ هَذَيْنِ إلهَيْنِ   حَاشَاي حَاشَاي مِنْ إثْباتِ اثنَيْنِ
هُوِيّةٌ لَكَ فِيَّ لا يَأتِيَنْ أبَداً   كُلِّي عَلَى الكُلِّ تَلْبيسٌ بِوَجْهَيْنِ
فأينَ ذَاتُكَ عَنّي حَيْثُ كُنْتُ أرَى   فَقَدْ تَبَيَّنَ ذَاتِي حَيْثُ لا أينَ
وأيْنَ وَجْهُكَ مَقْصُودٌ بناظِرَتِي   فِي نَاظِرِ القَلْبِ أمْ في نَاظِرِ العَيْنِ
بَيْنِي وَبَيْنَكَ أَنِّي يُزاحِمُنِي   فَارْفَعْ بِأنَّكَ أَنِّي مِنَ البَيْنِ

١٩

رَأَيْتُ رَبِّي بِعَيْنِ قَلْبِي   فَقُلْتُ مَنْ أنْتَ قَالَ أنْتَ
فَلَيْسَ لِلأَيْنِ مِنْكَ أيْنٌ   وَلَيْسَ أيْنٌ بِحَيْثُ أنْتَ
وَلَيْسَ لِلْوَهْمِ مِنْكَ وَهْمٌ   فَيَعْلَمُ الوَهْمُ أيْنَ أنْتَ
أنْتَ الّذِي حُزْتَ كُلَّ أيْنٍ   بِنَحْوِ لاَ أيْنَ فَأَيْنَ أنْتَ

20

O Secret of my secret, so subtle, Thou art veiled
From all imaginations of all beings that have life,
Yet outwardly, inwardly, Thou manifestest
Thyself in every thing to every thing.
Ignorance it were that I should proffer Thee my pleas,
Enormity of doubt, excess of impotence!
Sum of Totality, other than me Thou art not:
How then shall I plead for myself unto myself?[31]

21

For the Lights of religion's Light are Lights in men,
For the Secret, Secrets in secret depths of souls,
And for Being, in beings, is a Being that saith 'Be'.
Reserved for it my heart is, guided, and chosen.
O ponder what I say with the Intellect's eye.
Keen is the Intellect of hearing and of insight.[32]

22

Diverse longings had my soul,
But seeing Thee hath made them one.
Mine envied now mine envier is,
And lord of men I have become
Since Thou becamest Lord of me.
They chided me because of Thee,
My friends and foes, in ignorance
How grievously I had been tried.
Their world and their religion I
Have left to men, for Thy love's sake,
O my religion and my world.[33]

٢٠

يـا سِرَّ سِرِّي تَـدِقُّ حـتّى تَخْفَـىٰ عَـلَى وَهْـمِ كُلِّ حَيّ
وظَـاهِـراً بَـاطِـنـاً تَجَـلَّى في كُلِّ شَيْءٍ لِـكُلِّ شَئ
إنِ اعْـتِـذَارِي إلَيْـك جَـهْلٌ وعِـظْـمَ شَـكِّي وَفَـرْطِ عِيّ
يا جُمْلَةَ الكُلِّ لَستَ غَيْرِي فَمَـا اعْـتِـذَارِي إذاً إلَيّ

٢١

لِأنوارِ نُورِ الدِّينِ في الْخَلْقِ أنْوارٌ وَلِـلسِرِّ في سِرِّ المُسِرِّينَ أسْرَارُ
ولِلكَوْنِ في الأكْوانِ كَوْنٌ مُكَوِّنٌ يُكِنُّ لَهُ قَلْبِي وَيُهْدَى وَيَخْتارُ
تَأمَّلْ بِعَيْنِ العَقْلِ مَا أنا وَاصِفٌ فَلِلْعَقْلِ أسْمَاعٌ وُعَاةٌ وأبْصَارُ

٢٢

كانَـتْ لِـقَـلْـبِي أهْـواءٌ مُـفَـرَّقَـةٌ
فَاسْتَجْمَعَتْ مُذْ رَأَتْكَ العَيْنُ أهْوَائِي
فَصَارَ يَحْسُدُنِي مَنْ كُنْتُ أحْسُدُهُ
وَصِرْتُ مَوْلَى الْوَرَى مُذْ صِرْتَ مَوْلاَئِي
مَا لاَمَنِي فِيكَ أحِبّائِي وأَعْدَائِي
إلاَّ لِغَفْلَتِهِمْ عَنْ عِظْمِ بَلْوَائِي
تَرَكْتُ لِلنَّاسِ دُنْيَاهُمْ ودِينَهُمُ
شَغْلاً بِحُبِّكَ يَا دِينِي وَدُنْيائِي

23

I swear by God, sun riseth not nor setteth,
But in each breath I breathe my love for Thee,
Nor go I e'er apart with friends for discourse
But Thou, as I sit with them, art my theme;
Nor dwell my thoughts on Thee, sadly or gladly,
But Thou art in my heart, I murmur Thee.
Nor have I mind to drink of water in thirst,
But I behold Thine image in the cup.
And could I come to Thee, then speed I would
Upon my face, or walking on my head.[34]

24

Within my heart Thou dwellst; therein, of Thee, are secrets.
Good be that house for Thee, nay, good Whom there Thou findest!
Therein no secret is but Thee, none that I know of.
Look with Thine Eye; doth any other dwell there?
The night of separation, be it long or short,
Mine intimate friend is hope of Thee, memory of Thee.
Well pleased am I if it should please Thee to destroy me,
For what Thy choice is, O my Slayer, that I choose.[35]

٢٣

وَاللهِ مَا طَلَعَتْ شَمْسٌ وَلاَ غَرُبَتْ
إلاَّ وحُبُّكَ مَقْرُونٌ بِأنفَاسِي
وَلاَ خَلَوْتُ إلىَ قَوْمٍ أُحَدِّثُهُمْ
إلاَّ وَأَنْتَ حَدِيثِي بَيْنَ جُلاَّسِي
وَلاَ ذَكَرْتُكَ مَحْزوناً وَلاَ فَرِحاً
إلاَّ وَأَنْتَ بِقَلْبِي بَيْنَ وُسْوَاسِي
وَلاَ هَمَمْتُ بِشُرْبِ الْمَاءِ مِنْ عَطَشٍ
إلاَّ رَأَيْتُ خَيَالاً مِنْكَ فِي الْكَاسِ
وَلَوْ قَدَرْتُ عَلَى الإتْيانِ جِئْتِكُمُ
سَعْياً عَلَى الْوَجْهِ أوْ مَشْياً عَلَى الرَّاسِ

٢٤

سَكَنْتَ قَلْبِي وَفِيهِ مِنْكَ أسْرَارٌ
فَلْتَهْنَأ الدَّارُ بَلْ فَلْيَهْنَأ الْجَارُ
مَا فِيهِ غَيْرُكَ مِنْ سِرٍّ عَلِمْتُ بِهِ
فَانْظُرْ بِعَيْنِكَ هَلْ فِي الدّارِ دَيَّارُ
وَلَيْلَةُ الْهَجْرِ إنْ طَالَتْ وإنْ قَصُرَتْ
فَمُؤنِسِي أَمَلٌ فِيهِ وَتَذْكَارُ
إنِّي لَرَاضٍ بِمَا يُرْضِيكَ مِنْ تَلَفِي
يَا قَاتِلِي وَلِمَا تَخْتَارُ أخْتَارُ

25

I wrote, yet wrote not unto Thee, but wrote
Unto my Spirit mine unwritten writ.
Twixt Thee as Spirit and him who loveth It
No difference is of I to Thee. And naught
Is written but it goeth, from Thee proceeding,
To Thee, answering itself, no answer needing.[36]

26

O thou who blamest me my love for Him,
How harsh thou art; but if thou didst but know
How I have been enriched by Him thou wouldst not blame me.
Men have their pilgrimage, and I have mine
Unto my Guest within. They offer beasts
In sacrifice; I offer my heart's blood.
A folk there is whose rounds are not on foot:
Round God they go, absolved from round His House.[37]

27

Earnest for truth, I thought on the religions:
They are, I found, one root with many a branch.
Therefore impose on no man a religion,
Lest it should bar him from the firm-set root.
Let the root claim him, a root wherein all heights
And meanings are made clear, for him to grasp.[38]

٢٥

كَتَبْتُ وَلَمْ أَكْتُبْ إِلَيْكَ وإِنَّما كَتَبْتُ إِلَى رُوحِي بِغَيْرِ كِتَابِ
وَذَلِكَ أَنَّ الرُّوحَ لاَفَرْقَ بَيْنَها وَبَيْنَ مُحِبِّيها بِفَصْلِ خِطَابِ
وَكُلُّ كِتَابٍ صَادِرٍ مِنْكَ وَارِدٌ إِلَيْكَ بِلاَ رَدِّ الجَوابِ جَوَابِ

٢٦

يَا لائِمي فِي هَوَاهُ كَمْ تَلُومُ فَلَوْ
عَرَفْتَ مِنْهُ الَّذِي عُنِّيتُ لَمْ تَلُمِ
لِلنّاسِ حَجٌّ وَلِي حَجٌّ إلى سَكَنِي
تُهْدَى الأَضَاحِي وأُهْدِي مُهْجَتِي وَدَمِي
تَطوفُ بِالْبَيْتِ قَوْمٌ لا بِجَارِحَةٍ
بِاللّهِ طَافُوا فَأَغْنَاهُمْ عَنِ الحَرَمِ

٢٧

تَفَكَّرْتُ فِي الأَدْيَانِ جِدَّ تَحَقُّقٍ فَأَلْفَيْتُها أَصْلاً لَهُ شُعَباً جَمّا
فَلا تَطْلُبَنْ لِلْمَرْءِ دِيناً فَإِنَّهُ يُصَدُّ عَنِ الأَصْلِ الوَثِيقِ وإِنَّما
يُطَالِبُهُ أَصْلٌ يُعَبِّرُ عِنْدَهُ جَمِيعَ المَعَالِي وَالمَعَانِي فَيَفْهَمَا

28

I clasp with all my being all Thy Love.
Thou art my Sanctuary: Thou showest me Thee,
As if Thou wert within me. Turn I my heart
To other than Thee, I see naught but an alien,
Seeing thereby mine intimate ease with Thee.
Here Thou beholdest me in the prison of life,
Hemmed round by men, so snatch me thence, to Thee.[39]

29

What on earth so empty is of Thee
That they should rise to see Thee in Heaven?
Thou seest them look at Thee bedazzled:
They see Thee not, such is their blindness.[40]

30

Left me Thou hast, but hast not left my conscience,
Wherein Thou art my gladness and my joy.
When Thou didst go, gone was Thy going from me,
And absence presence is become for me
For Thou art in my secret depth of thought,
Hidden beyond imagining in my conscience.
Truly Thou art mine intimate by day,
At dark my boon conversor through the night.[41]

31

Thy place within my heart the whole heart is.
No room for creatures in that place of Thine.
Twixt skin and bone my spirit Thee hath wedged.
So what then could I do if I should lose Thee?[42]

٢٨

حَوَيْتُ بِكُلِّي كُلَّ حُبِّكَ يا قُدْسِي
أُكَاشِفُنِي حَتَّى كَأَنَّكَ فِي نَفْسِي
أُقَلِّبُ قَلْبِي فِي سِواكَ فَلاَ أَرَى
سِوَى وَحْشَتِي مِنْهُ وَمِنْكَ بِهِ أُنْسِي
فَهَا أَنَا فِي حَبْسِ الْحَياةِ مُجَمَّعٌ
مِنَ الإنْسِ فاقْبِضْنِي إِلَيْكَ مِنَ الْحَبْسِ

٢٩

وأيُّ الأرْضِ تَخْلُو مِنْكَ حَتَّى   تَعَالَوْا يَطْلُبونَكَ في السَّماءِ
تَرَاهُمْ يَنْظُرونَ إِلَيْكَ جَهْراً   وَهُمْ لاَ يُبْصِرُونَ مِنَ الْعَمَاءِ

٣٠

غِبْتَ وَمَا غِبْتَ عَنْ ضَمِيرِي   وَصِرْتَ فَرْحَتِي وَسُرُورِي
وانْفَصَلَ الفَصْلُ بِافْتِرَاقٍ   فَصَارَ فِي غَيْبَتِي حُضُورِي
فَأَنْتَ فِي سِرِّ غَيْبِ هَمِّي   أَخْفَى مِنَ الوَهْمِ فِي ضَمِيرِي
تُؤْنِسُنِي بِالنَّهارِ حَقّاً   وَأَنْتَ عِنْدَ الدُّجَى سَمِيرِي

٣١

مَكانُكَ فِي قَلْبِي هُوَ القَلْبُ كُلُّهُ
فَلَيْسَ لِخَلْقٍ فِي مَكَانِكَ مَوْضِعُ
وَحَطَّتْكَ رُوحِي بَيْنَ جِلْدِي وأَعْظُمِي
فَكَيْفَ تُرَانِي إِنْ فَقَدْتُكَ أَصْنَعُ

32

Thy Heart is that wherein a Name of Thine
Lies hidden, unseen by light, unseen by darkness,
And when I see Thy Face's Light, then I behold
A Mystery: That, That is the whole of Goodness,
All Excellence and all Munificence.
Take then, Beloved, my word; Thou knowest it,
The Tablet knoweth it not, nor yet the Pen.[43]

33

He am I whom I love, He whom I love is I,
Two Spirits in one single body dwelling.
So seest thou me, then seest thou Him,
And seest thou Him, then seest thou Us.[44]

34

Thy Spirit with my spirit mingled is,
Even as amber mingled is with musk
In blended perfumes. So, if aught Thee touch,
It toucheth me. Thus art Thou I inseparably.[45]

٣٢

قَلْبُكَ شَيْءٌ وفِيهِ مِنْكَ اسْمُ
لاَ النُّورُ يَدْرِي بِهِ كَلاَّ وَلاَ الظُّلَمُ
وَنورُ وَجْهِكَ سِرٌّ حِينَ أَشْهَدُهُ
هَذَا هُوَ الْجُودُ وَالإِحْسَانُ وَالكَرَمُ
فَخُذْ حَدِيثِي حُبِّي أَنْتَ تَعْلَمُهُ
لاَ اللّوْحُ يَعْلَمُهُ حَقّاً وَلاَ القَلَمُ

٣٣

أَنَا مَنْ أَهْوَى وَمَنْ أَهْوَى أَنَا   نَحْنُ رُوحَانِ حَلَلْنَا بَدَنَا
فَإِذَا أَبْصَرْتَنِي أَبْصَرْتَهُ   وَإِذَا أَبْصَرْتَهُ أَبْصَرْتَنَا

٣٤

جُبِلَتْ رُوحُكَ فِي رُوحِي كَمَا   تُجْبَلُ العَنْبَرُ بِالمِسْكِ الفَتِق
فَإِذا مَسَّكَ شَيْءٌ مَسَّنِي   فَإِذَا أَنْتَ أَنَا لاَ نَفْتَرِق

7

Abū Bakr Dulaf ibn Jaḥdar ash-Shiblī of Baghdad

(d. 334 AH/946 AD)

Shiblī was only three years younger than Ḥallāj but he outlived him by over twenty years. He also knew Sumnūn well and was himself over sixty years when Sumnūn died. One has the impression that Shiblī was possessed of a most poetical psychic substance, a soul that was often as it were on the verge of poetry, and it could also be said that he was something of a wit, if this word can be used in a purely spiritual sense. The readers will see what we have in mind from single lines (two lines in English) that would flash out of him from time to time. Nor is this gift of his altogether unrelated to an eloquence in virtue of which we owe him, amongst other things, a masterly definition of the Sufi norm of asceticism, 'the turning away of the heart from things unto the Lord of things'.

35

A fair apparel of patience I will don,
Longer and longer for vigil make my nights.
Unwillingly patient, not yet willing am I,
But little by little my soul I seek to enlist.[46]

36

Said my friend: 'How now is Thy patience with them?'[47]
So I said: 'Is there patience, to be asked of, how it is?
Fiercer than fire is love's heat in my heart,
Sweeter than piety, and sharper than the sword.'[48]

37

One day a cloud from Thee o'ershadowed us,
Dazzled us with its lightning, but held back its rain;
And its darkness cleareth not away, for the eager to despair,
Nor cometh the downpour for the thirsty to drink.[49]

38

He looked on me, then let me see
The wonders of His Care for me.
On fire I was, which made my heart
Melt, when His Presence drew apart.
Yet absent He is not, that I might take
To memory for consolation's sake,
Nor turned away, that I might absent be.[50]

٣٥

سَألْبَسُ لِلصَّبْرِ ثَوْباً جَمِيلاً وَأُدْرِجُ لَيْلِي لَيْلاً طَوِيلاَ
وَأصْبِرُ بِالرَّغْمِ لاَ بِالرِّضَى أعَلِّلُ نَفْسِي قَلِيلاً قَلِيلاَ

٣٦

يَقُولُ خَلِيلِي كَيْفَ صَبْرُكَ عَنْهُمُ
فَقُلْتُ وَهَلْ صَبْرٌ فَيُسْألُ عَنْ كَيْفِ
بِقَلْبِي هَوَىً أذْكَى مِنَ النَّارِ حَرُّهُ
وَأحْلَى مِنَ التَّقْوَى وَأمْضَى مِنَ السَّيْفِ

٣٧

أَظَلَّتْ عَلَيْنَا الْيَوْمَ مِنْكَ غَمَامَةٌ
أَضَاءَتْ لَنَا بَرْقاً وَأبْطَا رَشَاشُهَا
فَلاَ غَيْمُهَا يَجْلُو فَيَيْأسُ طَامِعٌ
وَلاَ غَيْثُهَا يَأتِي فَيُرْوِي عِطَاشُهَا

٣٨

رَآنِي فَأوْرَانِي عَجَائِبَ لُطْفِهِ فَهِمْتُ وَقَلْبِي بِالفُرَاقِ يَذُوبُ
فَلا غَائِبٌ عَنِّي فَأسْلو بِذِكْرِهِ وَلا هُوَ عَنِّي مُعْرِضٌ فَأغِيبُ

39

They said: 'Thou art mad for Laylā.' I said:[51]
'Madmen know only the easier part of love.'[52]

40

Not one heart didst Thou captive make in me;
Mine every limb a heart is unto Thee.[53]

41

Strange is my case, in strangeness I am all alone,
Unique amongst mankind, peer have I none.
My time, in Thee eternized, is Eternity,
And from myself Thou hast extinguished me.
So am I from createdness withdrawn, set free.[54]

42

Let the moons set or still be bright,
Ours is a full moon: in its sight
Full moons are humbled; for us its light
A splendour is by day and night.
No change of time can alter it.[55]

٣٩

قَالُوا جُنِنْتَ عَلَى لَيْلَى فَقُلْتُ لَهُمْ   الحُبُّ أَيْسَرُهُ مَا بالمَجانِينِ

٤٠

لَيْسَ مِنّي إلَيْكَ قَلْبٌ مُعَنَّى   كُلُّ عُضْوٍ مِنِّي إلَيْكَ قُلُوبُ

٤١

تَغَرَّبَ أَمْرِي فانْفَرَدْتُ بِغُرْبَتِي
فَصِرْتُ فَريداً فِي البَرِيَةِ أَوْحَدَا
تَسَرْمَدَ وَقْتِي فِيكَ فَهوَ مُسَرْمَدٌ
وَأَفْنَيْتَنِي عَنِّي فَصِرْتُ مُجَرَّدَا

٤٢

دَعِ الأَقْمارَ تَغْرُبْ أَوْ تُنِيرِ   لَنَا بَدْرٌ تُذَلُّ لَهُ البُدُورُ
لَنَا مِنْ نُورِهِ فِي كُلِّ وَقْتٍ   ضِيَاءٌ مَا تُغَيِّرُهُ الدُّهُورُ

8

Abū'l-ʿAbbās al-Qāsim as-Sayyārī of Marv

(d. 342 AH/953 AD)

The following much quoted poem, three lines in the original, appears to have been the result of a question often put to Sayyārī by would-be disciples as to how the novice should discipline his soul for the *Ṭarīqah*, that is, for the Sufi way.

Having answered the question on one occasion, and having summed up his answer in the words: 'A man is even as he shapes his soul to be', he then quoted very aptly these lines of his own which, we may suppose, had already been prompted by previous questions of the same kind as well as by his own personal spiritual experience.

43

Patiently pleasures I shunned till they shunned me.
I made my soul forsake them; steadfast she stood.
The soul's for man to make her as he would:
If fed, she seeks more; else, resigned she'll be.
Mine was an arrogant soul; but when she knew
Me resolute for humbleness, humble she grew.[56]

٤٣

صَبَرْتُ عَلَى اللَّذْاتِ حَتَّى تَوَلَّتْ　　وألزَمْتُ نَفْسِي هَجْرَهَا فاسْتَمَرَّت

ومَا النَّفْسُ إلاَّ حَيْثُ يَجْعَلُها الفَتَى　　فَإِنْ أُطْعِمَتْ تَاقَتْ وَإلاَّ تَسَلَّت

وَكانَتْ عَلَى الأَيَّامِ نَفْسًا عَزِيزَةً　　فَلَمَّا رَأتْ عَزْمِي عَلَى الذُّلِ ذَلَّت

9

ʿAbd al-ʿAzīz at-Tūnisī of Tunis

(d. 486 AH/1093 AD)

He studied doctrine and law under two Tunisian authorities, and then began to instruct others in what he himself had learnt, which was no doubt somewhat remote from Sufism. We know relatively little about him, but he seems to have had an experience not unlike that which, as we shall shortly see, changed the life of his younger contemporary, Abū Ḥāmid al-Ghazālī, who outlived him by nearly twenty years. The two experiences may have been very different as regards details, but what they have in common is that both men had established themselves as highly successful and much sought after teachers of the outer aspects of Islam, and both of them suddenly felt impelled to abandon that career and to devote themselves to the essence of the religion. Apart from this, although we know much about Abū Ḥāmid, we know very little about ʿAbd al-ʿAzīz. But in a certain sense it could be said that we know everything that needs to be known because of his legacy to us of a short poem which, with amazing eloquence and concision, may be said to sum up Sufism as regards both outlook and way, doctrine and method. Moreover, being what it is, it gives us the certitude that it could only have been written by a man who had found a Sufi Shaykh and had been initiated into one of the orders of Sufism. Let us add that it has an unmistakable ring of authority which inclines us to conclude that ʿAbd al-ʿAzīz had eventually come to have disciples of his own.

44

God hath slaves of insight: they
The world divorced have, lest she tempt them.
They thought on her, and when they knew her
To be no homeland for the living,
They took her as a sea, embarking
On best of deeds as boats to cross her.[57]

٤٤

إِنَّ لِلَّهِ عِبَاداً فُطُناً طَلَّقُوا الدُّنْيَا وَخافُوا الفِتَنا
فَكَّرُوا فِيهَا فَلَمَّا عَلِمُوا أَنَّهَا لَيْسَتْ لِحَيٍ وَطَنَا
جَعَلُوها لُجَّةً واتَّخَذُوا صَالِحَ الأَعْمَالِ فِيها سُفُنَا

10

Abū Ḥāmid Muḥammad al-Ghazālī of Baghdad

(d. 505 AH/1111 AD)

Having become one of the leading authorities of Baghdad as regards the outer aspects of Islam, he suddenly began to doubt the truth of religion, and this crisis, as he tells us, lasted for nearly two months. It was contact with a Sufi Shaykh that re-established his faith on an incomparably firmer basis than before; and his well known treatise, *The Saviour from Error* (*al-Munqidh min aḍ-Ḍalāl*), amounts to an affirmation that Sufism is indeed the heart of Islam. This treatise was followed by his longest and best known work, *The Revival of the Sciences of the Religion* (*Iḥyā' ʿUlūm ad-Dīn*), the purpose of which, one might say, is to awaken dormant spiritual ideals throughout the community as a whole. But not all his writings were written for everyone. His *Niche of Lights* (*Mishkāt al-Anwār*) is the work of a Sufi Shaykh written for the best of his disciples and, by extension, for the disciples of others at the same level. By contrast, the poem from which we will quote here the opening eight lines, sixteen in our translation, is quite literally for everybody, that is, for anyone who knows Arabic or the language of one of its translations, no matter what his or her religion might be. Presumably Ghazālī wrote it towards the end of his life, and it is said by some to have been found under his pillow after his death.

45

Say unto brethren when they see me dead,
And weep for me, lamenting me in sadness:
'Think ye I am this corpse ye are to bury?
I swear by God, this dead one is not I.
I in the Spirit am, and this my body
My dwelling was, my garment for a time.
I am a treasure: hidden I was beneath
This talisman of dust, wherein I suffered.
I am a pearl; a shell imprisoned me,
But leaving it, all trials I have left.
I am a bird, and this was once my cage;
But I have flown, leaving it as a token.
I praise God who hath set me free, and made
For me a dwelling in the heavenly heights.
Ere now I was a dead man in your midst,
But I have come to life, and doffed my shroud.'[58]

٤٥

قُلْ لإخْوانٍ رَأوْني مَيِّتاً　فَبَكَوْني وَرَثَوْا لِي حَزَنَا
أَتَظُنّونَ بِأنّي مَيْتُكُمْ　لَيْسَ ذَاكَ المَيِّتُ وَاللّٰهِ أَنَا
أَنَا فِي الصُّوَرِ وَهَذَا جَسَدِي　كَانَ بَيْتِي وقَمِيصِي زَمَنَا
أَنَا كَنْزٌ وَحِجَابِي طَلْسَمٌ　مِنْ تُرابٍ كَانَ لِي فِيهِ عَنَا
أَنَا دُرٌّ قَدْ حَوَاهُ صَدَفٌ　كُنْتُ مَمْحُوناً فَعِفْتُ المِحَنَا
أَنَا عُصْفُورٌ وَهَذَا قَفَصِي　طِرْتُ مِنْهُ وَبَقَى مُرْتَهَنَا
أَحْمَدُ اللّٰهَ الَّذِي خَلَّصَنِي　وَبَنَى لِي فِي المَعَالِي سَكَنَا
كُنْتُ قَبْلَ اليَوْمِ مَيّتاً بَيْنَكُمُ　فَحَيِيتُ وَخَلَعْتُ الكَفَنَا

11

Muḥyī'd-Dīn Muḥammad ibn ʿAlī Ibn ʿArabī of Andalusia

(d. 638 AH/1240 AD)

Ibn ʿArabī was brought up mainly in Seville, but after several visits to North-west Africa he had a vision at the age of thirty-three in which he received a Divine Command to go to the East. There, after much travelling and longer or shorter periods of rest in various places—Cairo, Mecca, Baghdad, Mosul, Konya, Aleppo and others—he finally settled in Damascus where he died at the age of seventy-five. He was one of the most prolific of all Sufi writers, and although much of what he wrote appears to have been lost, what survives has had an untold influence on Sufism ever since. He was recognised as a Saint in his life-time and even in his youth. Kings and princes courted him for his advice, which was implacably and fearlessly outspoken; and it was no doubt in the domain of personal contacts as well as through his writings, if not more, that he made himself felt during his life-time. A mosque was built over his much visited tomb in the sixteenth-century by the Ottoman Sultan Salīm I.

The spirituality of a Heaven-sent Messenger (*Rasūl*)—for example, Moses, Jesus, Muḥammad—is held to be incomparable. As to the subsidiary degree of Prophethood, every Messenger is thereby a Prophet (*Nabī*); but most Prophets are not Messengers, and it is recognised in Sufism that the greatest of the Saints, amongst whom the man we are speaking of must unquestionably be placed, are those who have realised the spiritual plenitude of Prophethood without having the prophetic function itself.

In Ibn ʿArabī yet again, as always at the summits of Sufism, we encounter the presence of ardent love side by side with the pure objectivity of the true intellectual. Of the five examples of his poetry given here, the first three are taken from the sixty-one mystical odes which, together with his own commentary, the poet himself placed in one volume under the title *Tarjumān al-ashwāq*, rendered by Nicholson as *The Interpreter of Desires.* I myself prefer the slightly non-literal *The Interpreter of Longings.* The first of our quotations is one of several examples of Ibn ʿArabī's readiness to exploit the fashions of his day and as it were to echo, by way of form, the pre-Islamic odes of lamentation for the departure of loved ones; but for him the loved ones are, needless to say, very different from those of the contemporary court poets and their more ancient models.

Nicholson gives good reasons for supposing that these odes were written in Mecca in 611 AH (1214 AD), and that in them the poet is looking back to a visit he had made there twelve years previously. During that visit, he had spent much time with a saintly authority on Traditions named Makīnu'd-Dīn who had become very dear to him, and the 'maiden of fourteen', who is the theme of our second quotation, was the daughter of this friend. We have no reason to suppose that he ever saw her again after that earlier visit, and when he returned in 611 her father was no longer alive. The poem in question can perhaps be considered central to the *Tarjumān* as a whole, for the poet in his preface gives us to understand, with regard to the maiden, that she is a blessed synthesis of the 'they' of our last quotation and of many others of these odes. He says: 'Whenever I mention a name in this book I always allude to her, and whenever I mourn over an abode I mean her abode.' In his commentary he stresses that fourteen, the number of the full moon, indicates 'the perfect soul'; and in connection with her name Niẓām, which he considers to be eloquently expressive of her incomparability, I feel that he would have applauded the following quotation which I venture to make from a great Sufi of the last century, disciple and successor of the already mentioned Shaykh Aḥmad al-ʿAlawī who gave him the name ʿIsā Nūr ad-Dīn, though he is known to us, from his remarkable books, as

Frithjof Schuon. In one of his yet unpublished texts, written especially for his disciples, he affirms that the perfection of human virtue is 'to be in harmonious confrontation with God'. Now can it not be said that the most eloquent worldly symbol of the relationship between God and man is the relationship between the two luminaries, the sun and the moon? The words 'moon' and 'man' are even etymologically connected; and it is on its fourteenth night, when it is full, *and only then*, that the moon is in harmonious confrontation with the sun. The name Niẓām, Harmony, thus enables the maiden of fourteen to personify most marvellously perfection of virtue.

As to the last of our three quotations from the *Tarjumān*, it consists of what are probably the most often quoted and most widely known lines of all Ibn ʿArabī's poetry. These are followed by two poems of his that are very different from anything else in this volume and also from each other, except that they are both, as we shall see, deliberately mysterious in their expression of transcendent truths.

46

Endurance went, and patience went, when they went.[59]
Gone, even they, tenants of mine inmost heart!
I asked where the riders rest at noon, was answered:
'They rest where the *shīḥ* and *bān* tree spread their fragrance.'[60]
So said I to the wind: 'Go and o'ertake them,
For they, even now, in the shade of the grove are biding,
And give them greetings of peace from a sorrowful man,
Whose heart sorroweth at severance from his folk.'[61]

47

There rose for me twixt Adhriʿāt and Buṣrā
A maiden of fourteen like a full moon.
Higher than time she stood in majesty,
Transcendent over it in pride and glory.
Each moon when it hath reached its plenitude
A waning suffereth to fulfil the month,
Save this: no movements hath she through the Signs
Nor maketh, being repeated, two[62] of One.
Treasury, thou, of blended fragrances,
Meadow that putteth forth spring herbs and flowers,
Beauty hath reached in thee her utmost end.
For others like to thee there is no room
In all the scope of what is possible.[63]

48

Receptive now my heart is for each form;
For gazelles pasture, for monks a monastery,
Temple for idols, Kaʿbah to be rounded,
Tables of Torah and script of Qur'ān.
My religion is love's religion: where'er turn
Her camels, that religion my religion is, my faith.
An example is set us by Bishr, lover
Of Hind and her sister, and likewise the loves
Of Qays and Laylā, of Mayya and Ghaylān.[64]

٤٦

بَانَ العَزَاءُ وَبَانَ الصَّبْرُ إذْ بَانُوا   بَانُوا وَهُمْ فِي سُوَيْدِ القَلْبِ سُكّانُ
سَأَلْتُهُمْ عَنْ مَقِيلِ الرَّكْبِ قِيلَ لَنَا   مَقِيلُهُمْ حَيْثُ فَاحَ الشِيحُ وَالْبَانُ
فَقُلْتُ لِلرِّيحِ سِيرِي والْحَقِي بِهِمُ   فإنَّهُمْ عِنْدَ ظِلِّ الأيْكِ قُطّانُ
وَبَلِّغِيهُمْ سَلاماً مِنْ أخِي شَجَنٍ   فِي قَلْبِهِ مِنْ فِرَاقِ القَوْمِ أشْجَانُ

٤٧

طَلَعَتْ بَيْنَ أذْرُعاتٍ وبُصْرى   بِنْتُ عَشْرٍ وَأرْبَعٍ لِيَ بَدْرَا
قَدْ تَعَالَتْ عَلَى الزَّمَانِ جَلالاً   وَتَسامَتْ عَلَيْهِ كِبْراً وفَخْرَا
كُلُّ بَدْرٍ إذا تَنَاهَى كَمَالاً   جَاءَهُ نَقْصُهُ لِيُكْمِلَ شَهْرَا
غَيْرَ هَذِي فَمَا لَهَا حَرَكَاتٌ   فِي بُروجٍ فَمَا تَشفَعُ وَتْرَا
حَقّةٌ أوْدَعَتْ عَبِيراً وَنَشْراً   رَوْضَةٌ أنْبَتَتْ رَبِيعاً وَزَهْرَا
انْتَهى الحُسْنُ فِيكِ أقْصَى مَدَاهُ   مَا لِوُسْعِ الإمْكانِ مِثْلُكِ أُخْرَى

٤٨

لَقَدْ صَارَ قَلْبِي قَابِلاً كُلَّ صُورَةٍ   فَمَرْعَى لِغُزلانٍ وَدِيرٌ لِرُهْبَانِ
وَبَيْتٌ لأوْثَانٍ وكَعْبَةُ طَايِفٍ   وَألْوَاحُ تَوْراةٍ وَمُصْحَفُ قُرآنِ
أَدِينُ بِدَيْنِ الحُبِّ أنّى تَوَجَّهَتْ   رَكائِبُهُ فَالدِّينُ دِينِي وإيمَانِي
لَنَا أُسْوَةٌ فِي بِشْرِ هِنْدٍ وَأُخْتِهَا   وَقَيْسٍ وَلَيْلَى ثُمَّ مَيٍّ وَغَيلانِ

49

Make thine ablution with the waters of the Unseen,[65]
If hast the secret; else, with earth or stone,[66]
And take as leader one whose leader thou'rt become,
And pray the dawn prayer in mid-afternoon.[67]
This is the gnostics' prayer; if of them thou be,
Then flood the land with waters of the sea.[68]

50

We were letters, exalted! not yet uttered,
Held aloft in the keep of the Highest of Summits,
I Therein am Thou, and we are Thou,
And Thou art He, and All is in He is He—
Ask of any that so far hath reached.[69]

٤٩

تَوَضَّأْ بِمَاءِ الغَيْبِ إنْ كُنْتَ ذَا سِرٍّ
وإلاَّ تَيَمَّمْ بالصَّعِيدِ أوِ الصَّخْرِ
وَقَدِّمْ إمَاماً صِرْتَ أنْتَ إمَامَهُ
وَصَلِّ صَلاَةَ الفَجْرِ في أوَّلِ الْعَصْرِ
فَهَذِى صَلاَةُ العَارِفِينَ بِرَبِّهِمْ
فَإنْ كُنْتَ مِنْهُمْ فَانْضحِ الْبَرَّ بالبَحْرِ

٥٠

كُنَّا حُرُوفاً عَالِياتٍ لَمْ نُقَلْ
مُتَعَلِّقاتٍ في ذُرى أعْلَى القُلَلْ
أنَا أنْتَ فِيهِ وَنَحْنُ أنْتَ وَأنْتَ هُوَ
وَالكُلُّ في هُوَ هُوَ فَسَلْ عَمَّنْ وَصَلْ

12

Sharafu'd-Dīn ʿUmar Ibn al-Fāriḍ of Egypt

(d. 633 AH/1235 AD)

Ibn al-Fāriḍ, like his Andalusian contemporary Ibn ʿArabī, was also revered as a Saint in his life-time, and his tomb at the foot of the Muqattam range of hills is held to be one of the seven holy places of Cairo. But unlike Ibn ʿArabī he wrote only poetry; and there are many who consider him to be the greatest of all Arab poets. We have mentioned his honorific title 'the Sultan of the Yearners' in connection with that of Sumnūn, 'the Lover', and we have pointed out that neither title must be taken to imply a departure from the Sufi norm of 'Love within the framework of Gnosis.' By extension, in view of our first and longest quotation from the poems of Ibn al-Fāriḍ, namely *The Wine-Song* (*al-Khamriyyah*), let us point out that wine is here the symbol of Gnosis and Love in their Essential Oneness, the Divine Radiance whereby all things exist and the Divine Attraction whereby all existence is reabsorbed into its Principle. The Gnosis-Love is both Transcendent and Immanent; its Subject as well as its Object is God. Being Absolute, pure Wine is only accessible to man in virtue of the Divine Self in the depth of his heart. It is also likened to the sun, and the full moon, its cup, is the Logos, the Spirit of Muhammad (*ar-Rūḥ al-Muḥammadī*), and by extension the Spiritual Master, the Shaykh. The crescent is a disciple of promise who is 'growing' towards the perfection of plenitude. The tavern is the *Zāwiyah* where the Sufi gatherings are held, and the people of the tavern are the initiates of the *Ṭarīqah*, that is, the order or brotherhood. Each generation of Sufis has lamented the spiritual decadence of the present as compared with the past. The poet complains of his times by dwelling on the absence or hiddenness of the wine.

Like some others of our poets, Ibn al-Fāriḍ was on his way to becoming an expert in outer aspects of Islam, but at his contact with Sufism such activities were replaced by periods of solitude on the Muqattam hills and in the desert beyond. He nonetheless remained the much loved centre of a family who greatly treasured his illuminating presence and also his poems. One of the oldest manuscripts of these is in the hand of a grandson of his, the son of one of his daughters.

Although Ibn al-Fāriḍ lived in Egypt for most of his life he spent over ten years in Arabia, mainly in Mecca, returning to Cairo because he miraculously heard the voice of his Shaykh who was on his death-bed, bidding him come. Later he made a second visit to Arabia, taking with him his sons Muḥammad and ʿAbd ar-Raḥmān. Their visit to the holy places happened to coincide with the visit of another great Sufi Shaykh, Shihāb ad-Dīn ʿUmar as-Suhrawardī of Baghdad, who invested each of the two younger men with a cloak, *khirqah.* This was probably not an initiation in the full sense for they must almost certainly have been already the disciples of their father. It would have been what is known as an 'initiation of blessing' (*bayʿ at at-tabarruk*), which, in this particular case, would have served indirectly as a noble gesture of great good will towards the poet himself. Not long afterwards they returned to Egypt, and Ibn al-Fāriḍ died in Cairo some four years later.

51

The Wine–Song[70]

Rememb'ring the belovèd, wine we drink
Which drunk had made us ere the vine's creation.
A sun it is; the full moon is its cup;
A crescent hands it round; how many stars
Shine forth from it the moment it be mixed!
But for its fragrance ne'er had I been guided
Unto its tavern; but for its resplendence
Imagining could no image make of it.
Time its mere gasp hath left; hidden it is.
Like secrets pent in the intelligence,
Yet if it be remembered in the tribe,[71]
All become drunk—no shame on them nor sin.
Up hath it fumed from out the vessel's dregs.
Nothing is left of it, only a name;
Yet if that name but enter a man's mind,
Gladness shall dwell with him and grief depart.
Had the boon revellers gazed upon its seal,[72]
That seal, without the wine, had made them drunk.
Sprinkle a dead man's grave with drops of it,
His spirit would return, his body quicken.
If in the shadow of the wall where spreads
Its vine they laid a man, mortally sick,
Gone were his sickness; and one paralysed,
Brought near its tavern, would walk; the dumb would speak,
Did he its savour recollect. Its fragrance,

الخَمرِيَّه

شَرِبْنَا عَلَى ذِكْرِ الحَبِيبِ مُدَامَةً
سَكِرْنَا بِهَا مِنْ قَبْلِ أَنْ يُخْلَقَ الكَرْمُ
لَهَا البَدْرُ كَأْسٌ وَهِيَ شَمْسٌ يُدِيرُهَا
هِلالٌ وَكَمْ يَبْدُو إذا مُزِجَتْ نَجْمُ
وَلَوْلا شَذَاها مَا إهْتَدَيْتُ لِحانِها
وَلَوْلاَ سَنَاهَا مَا تَصَوَّرَهَا الوَهْمُ
ولَمْ يُبْقِ مِنْها الدَّهْرُ غَيْرَ حُشاشَةٍ
كأنّ خَفَاها في صُدورِ النُّهَى كَتْمُ
فَإنْ ذُكِرَتْ في الحَيّ أصْبحَ أهْلُهُ
نَشاوَى وَلا عَارٌ عَلَيْهِمُ وَلاَ إثْمُ
وَمِنْ بَيْنِ أحْشاءِ الدِنَانِ تَصاعَدَتْ
وَلَمْ يَبْقَ مِنْها في الحَقِيقَةِ إلاَّ اسْمُ
وإنْ خَطَرَتْ يَوْماً عَلَى خَاطِرِ امْرِىءٍ
أقامَتْ بِهِ الأفْراحُ وارْتَحَلُ الهَمُّ
ولَوْ نَظَرَ النُّدْمَانُ خَتْمَ إنَائِهَا
لأسْكَرَهُمْ مِنْ دُونِهَا ذَلِكَ الخَتْمُ
ولوْ نَضَحُوا مِنْها ثَرَى قَبْرِ مَيِّتٍ
لَعادَتْ إليْهِ الرُّوحُ وانْتَعَشَ الجِسْمُ
ولوْ طَرَحُوا في فَيْءِ حَائِطِ كَرْمِها
عَلِيلاً وَقَدْ أشْفَى لَفَارَقَهُ السُّقْمُ
ولوْ قَرَّبوا مِنْ حَانِها مُقعَداً مَشَى
ويَنْطِقُ مِنْ ذِكْرَى مَذاقَتِها البُكْمُ

If wafted through the East, even in the West,
Would free, for one berheumed, his sense of smell;
And he who stained his palm, clasping its cup,
Could never, star in hand, be lost by night.
Unveil it like a bride in secrecy[73]
Before one blind from birth: his sight would dawn.
Decant it, and the deaf would hearing have.
If riders rode out for its native earth,[74]
And one of them were bit by snake, unharmed
By poison he. If the enchanter traced[75]
The letters of its name on madman's brow,
That script would cure him of his lunacy;
And blazoned on the standard of a host,[76]
Its name would make all men beneath it drunk.
In virtue the boon revellers it amends,
Makes perfect. Thus by it the irresolute
Is guided to the path of firm resolve.
Bountiful he, whose hand no bounty knew;
And he that never yet forbore forbeareth,
Despite the goad of anger. The tribe's dunce,
Could he but kiss its filter, by that kiss
Would win the sense of all its attributes.
'Describe it, well thou knowest how it is',
They bid me. Yea, its qualities I know:
Not water and not air nor fire nor earth,
But purity for water, and for air
Subtlety, light for fire, spirit for earth—
Excellencies that guide to extol its good
All who would tell of it, and excellent
Their prose in praise of it, excellent their verse.
So he that knew not of it can rejoice[77]
To hear it mentioned, as Nuʿm's lover doth
To hear her name, whenever Nuʿm is named.
Before all beings, in Eternity
It is, ere yet was any shape or trace.

ولوْ عَبِقَتْ في الشَّرْقِ أنْفَاسُ طِيبِها
وَفي الغَرْبِ مَزْكُومٌ لَعَادَ لَهُ الشَّمُّ
ولوْ جُلِيَتْ سِرّاً عَلَى أكْمَهٍ غَدَا
بَصِيراً وَمِنْ رَاووقِهَا تَسْمَعُ الصُّمُّ
ولـوْ رَسَمَ الرَّاقِي حُرُوفَ اسْمِهَـا
عَلَى جَبِينِ مُصَابٍ جُنَّ أبْرَأَهُ الرَّسْمُ
وَفَوْقَ لِوَاءِ الجَيْشِ لوْ رُقِمَ اسْمُهَا
لأسْكَرَ مَنْ تَحْتَ اللِّوَا ذَلكَ الرَّقْمُ
تُهَذِّبُ أخْلاقَ النَدَامى فَيَهْتَدي
بِهَا لِطَرِيقِ العَزْمِ مَنْ لاَ لَهُ عَزْمُ
وَيَكْرُمُ مَنْ لَمْ يَعْرِفِ الجُودَ كَفُّهُ
وَيَحْلُمُ عِنْدَ الغَيْظِ مَنْ لا لَهُ حِلْمُ
وَلَوْ نَالَ فَدْمُ القَوْمِ لَثْمَ فِدَامِهَا
لأَكْسَبَهُ مَعْنَى شَمَائِلِها اللَثْمُ
يَقُولُونَ لِي صِفْها فأَنْتَ بِوَصْفِهَا
خَبيرٌ أجَلْ عِنْدِي بأوْصافِها عِلْمُ
صَفَاءٌ ولا مَاءٌ ولُطْفٌ ولا هَوَاً
ونُورٌ ولا نَارٌ ورُوحٌ ولا جِسْمُ
مَحَاسِنُ تَهدِي المَادِحِينَ لِوَصْفِهَا
فَيَحْسُنُ فِيهَا مِنهُمُ النَّثْرُ وَالنَّظْمُ
وَيَطْرَبُ مَنْ لَمْ يَدْرِها عِنْدَ ذِكْرِهَا
كَمُشتاقِ نُعْمٍ كُلَّمَا ذُكِرَتْ نُعْمُ
أَقدَمَ كُلَّ الكَائِنَاتِ حَدِيثُهَا
قَدِيماً ولا شَكْلٌ هُنَاكَ ولا رَسْمُ

Through it things were, then it by them was veiled,
Wisely, from him who understandeth not.
My spirit loved it, was made one with it,
But not as bodies each in other merge.
Wine without vine: Adam my father is.
Vine without wine, vine mothereth it and me.[78]
Vessels are purer for the purity
Of truths which are their content, and those truths
Are heightened by the vessels being pure.[79]
Things have been diff'renced, and yet all is One:
Our spirits wine are, and our bodies vine.[80]
Before it no before is, after it
No after is; absolute its privilege
To be before all afters. Ere time's span
Its pressing was, and our first father's age[81]
Came afterwards—parentless orphan it!
They tell me: 'Thou hast drunk iniquity'.
Not so, I have but drunk what not to drink
Would be for me iniquitous indeed.
Good for the monastery folk, that oft
They drunken were with it, yet drank it not,
Though fain would drink. But ecstasy from it
Was mine ere I existed, shall be mine
Beyond my bones' decaying. Drink it pure!
But if thou needs must have it mixed, 'twere sin
To shun mouth-water from the Loved One's lips.[82]
Go seek it in the tavern; bid it unveil
To strains of music. They offset its worth,

وَقَامَتْ بِهَا الأَشْيَاءُ ثَمَّ لِحِكْمَةٍ
بِهَا احْتَجَبَتْ عَنْ كُلِّ مَنْ لا لَهُ فَهْمُ
وَهَامَتْ بِهَا رُوحِي بِحَيْثُ تَمَازَجَا
أحاداً ولا جِرْمٌ تَخَلَّلَهُ جِرْمُ
فَخَمْرٌ ولا كَرْمٌ وآدَمُ لِي أَبٌ
وكَرْمٌ ولا خَمْرٌ وَلِي أُمُّهَا أُمُّ
وَلُطْفُ الأَوَانِي في الحَقِيقَةِ تابِعٌ
لِلُطْفِ المَعَانِي والمَعانِي بِهَا تَنْمُو
وَقَدْ وَقَعَ التَّفْرِيقُ والكُلُّ وَاحِدٌ
فأرْوَاحُنا خَمْرٌ وأشْباحُنا كَرْمُ
ولا قَبْلَها قَبْلٌ ولا بَعْدَ بَعْدِها
وَقَبْلِيَّةُ الأبْعَادِ فَهْىَ لَهَا حَتْمُ
وَعَصْرُ المَدَى مِنْ قَبْلِهِ كانَ عَصْرَها
وَعَهْدُ أبِينَا بِعْدَها وَلَهَا اليُتْمُ
وقَالوا شَرِبْتَ الإِثْمَ كَلاَّ وَإنَّمَا
شَرِبْتُ الَّتِي في تَرْكِها عِنْدِيَ الإثْمُ
هَنيئاً لأهْلِ الدَّيْرِ كَمْ سَكِرُوا بِهَا
وَما شَرِبوا مِنْهَا وَلَكِنَّهُمْ هَمُّوا
وَعِنْدِي مِنْها نَشْوَةٌ قَبْلَ نَشْأتِي
مَعِي أبداً تَبْقَى وَإنْ بَلِيَ العَظْمُ
عَلَيْكَ بِها صِرْفاً وإنْ شِئْتَ مَزْجَها
فَعَدْلُكَ عَنْ ظُلْمِ الحَبِيبِ هُوَ الظُّلْمُ
فَدُونَكَها في الحَانِ واسْتَجْلِها بِهِ
عَلَى نَغَمِ الألْحَانِ فَهْيَ بِها غُنْمُ

For wine and care dwelt never in one place,
Even as woe with music cannot dwell.
Be drunk one hour with it, and thou shalt see
Time's whole age as thy slave, at thy command.
He hath not lived here, who hath sober lived,
And he that dieth not drunk hath missed the mark.
With tears then let him mourn himself, whose life
Hath passed, and he no share of it hath had.

52

Give me excess of love and so increase me
In marvelling at Thee; and mercy have
Upon a heart for Thee by passion seared.
And when I ask of Thee that I may see Thee
Even as Thou art, in Thy reality,
Say not: *Thou shalt not see*, but let me see.[83]
Heart, thou didst promise patience in love of them.
Take heed, and be not troubled, be not anguished.
Verily love is life, so die in love,
And claim thy right to die, all sins forgiven.
Tell those before me and those after me,
And whoso witness of my sorrow was:
Learn from me, my example take, and hear me,
And tell mankind the story of my love.
Alone with the Belovèd I have been:
A secret subtler than wind's lightest breath,
When on the night it steals, between us passed;
He granted to my gaze a longed for sight,
Whence I, till then unknown, illustrious am.

فَمَا سَكَنَتْ وَالهَمَّ يَوْمَاً بِمَوضِعٍ
كَذٰلِكَ لَمْ يَسْكُنْ مَعَ النَّغَمِ الغَمُّ
وفي سَكْرَةٍ مِنْها وَلوْ عُمْرُ ساعَةٍ
تَرَى الدَّهْرَ عَبْدَاً طائِعاً وَلَكَ الحُكْمُ
فَلاَ عَيْشَ في الدُّنْيَا لِمَنْ عَاشَ صَاحِياً
ومَنْ لَمْ يَمُتْ سُكْرَاً بِها فاتَهُ الحَزْمُ
عَلَى نَفْسِهِ فَلَبَيْكِ مَنْ ضَاعَ عُمْرُهُ
وَلَيْسَ لَهُ فِيها نَصِيبٌ ولا سَهْمُ

٥٢

زِدْنِي بِفَرْطِ الحُبِّ فِيكَ تَحَيُّرَا
وَارْحَمْ حَشىً بِلَظَى هَوَاكَ تَسَعَّرَا
وَإِذا سَأَلْتُكَ أَنْ أَرَاكَ حَقِيقَةً
فَاسْمَحْ وَلا تَجْعَلْ جَوَابِي لَنْ تَرَى
يَاقَلْبُ أَنْتَ وَعَدْتَنِي في حُبِهِم
صَبْرًا فَحَاذِرْ أَنْ تَضِيقَ وَتَضْجَرَا
قُلْ لِلَّذينَ تَقَدَّمُوا قَبْلِي وَمَنْ
بَعْدي وَمَنْ أَضْحَى لأَشْجانِي يَرَى
عَنِّي خُذوا وَبِيَ اقْتَدُوا وَلِيَ اسْمَعُوا
وَتَحَدَّثوا بِصَبَابَتِي بَيْنَ الوَرَى
وَلَقَدْ خَلَوْتُ مَعَ الحَبِيبِ وَبَيْنَنا
سِرٌّ أَرَقُّ مِنَ النَّسِيمِ إِذا سَرَى
وَأَبَاحَ طَرْفِي نَظْرَةً أَمَّلْتُها
فَغَدَوْتُ مَعْروفاً وَكُنْتُ مُنَكَّرَا

Between His Beauty and His Majesty
I marvelled, and my state of marvelling
Was like an eloquent tongue that spake of me.
Turn then thy looks unto His Countenance,
To find the whole of beauty lineate there.
All beauty, if it gathered were and made
One perfect form, beholding Him, would say:
There is no god but God; God is most great.[84]

53

Had they recalled his face's loveliness to Jacob,
From his remembrance Joseph's beauty would have vanished;[85]
Or if Job even in his sleep had seen him come
A visitant, the sooner had his plague been cured.
To him when he is manifest and face to face
Every full moon and every lesser form do lean.
His virtues are perfections: had he given his light
To the full moon, it never would have been eclipsed.
Said I 'all love for thee is in me', he would say:
'Loveliness is mine; the whole of beauty is in me.'
For all the art of those who would describe his beauty,
Time shall run out, and never he be full described.[86]

54

Showing Herself, She showed forth Being to mine eye
So that I saw Her in my seeing's every sight.
Her showing made me witness mine own hidden deep:
There, once my secret was displayed, I found me Her.

فَدُهِشْتُ بَيْنَ جَمَالِهِ وَجَلَالِهِ
وَغَدَا لِسَانُ الْحَالِ عَنِّى مُخْبِرَا

فَأَدِرْ لِحَاظَكَ فِي مَحَاسِنِ وَجْهِهِ
تَلْقَى جَمِيعَ الْحُسْنِ فِيهِ مُصَوَّرَا

لَوْ أَنَّ كُلَّ الْحُسْنِ يَكْمُلُ صُورَةً
وَرَآهُ كَانَ مُهَلِّلاً وَمُكَبِّرَا

٥٣

لَوْ أَسْمَعُوا يَعْقُوبَ ذِكْرَ مَلَاحَةٍ
فِي وَجْهِهِ نَسِيَ الْجَمَالَ الْيُوسُفِي

أَوْ لَوْ رَآهُ عَائِداً أَيُّوبُ فِي
سِنَةِ الْكَرَى قِدَماً مِنَ الْبَلْوَى شُفِي

كُلُّ الْبُدُورِ إِذَا تَجَلَّى مُقْبِلاً
تَصْبُوا إِلَيْهِ وَكُلُّ قَدٍّ أَهْيَفِ

كَمُلَتْ مَحَاسِنُهُ فَلَوْ أَهْدَى السَّنا
لِلْبَدْرِ عِنْدَ تَمَامِهِ لَمْ يُخْسَفِ

إِنْ قُلْتُ عِنْدِي فِيكَ كُلُّ صَبَابَةٍ
قَالَ الْمَلَاحَةُ لِي وَكُلُّ الْحُسْنِ فِي

٥٤

جَلَتْ فِي تَجَلِّيهَا الْوُجُودَ لِنَاظِرِي
فَفِي كُلِّ مَرْئِيٍّ أَرَاهَا بِرُؤْيَةِ

وَأُشْهِدْتُ غَيْبِي إِذْ بَدَتْ فَوَجَدْتُنِي
هُنَالِكَ إِيَّاهَا بِجَلْوَةِ خَلْوَتِي

So mine existence in my seeing vanishèd,
Seeing's existence I sloughed off, effacing it,
And I embraced the Object I did contemplate,
With seeing effaced in what it saw. This state I kept
For my sobriety after my drunkenness.
Thus once effaced, ev'n sober I am none but She:
Her shining forth my robing was of self with self.
Since that not two is, I must be described as She,
And Her appearance, since we are but one, is mine.
Thus I, if She be summoned, am the answerer,
And She my summoner answereth with 'here am I',
And if She maketh utterance it is I that speak,
And She, whene'er I tell a tale, the teller is.
Gone from between us is the one-to-other's 'Thou';
Gone, at its going, I from separation's sect.[87]

55

From separation's error separate thyself,
Seek to be joined, reap joining's fruit, the guidance
Of that good company that vied for union.
Beauty is absolute: declare it; count it not
Relative, lured by glitter of some ornament.
Every fair youth, every fair maid their beauty have
On loan from Hers: She was it that Qays loved
In Lubnā, every yearning lover loved but Her.[88]
E'en as Majnūn loved Laylā and Kuthayyir ʿAzzah.[89]

وَطَاحَ وُجُوْدِي في شُهُودِي وَبِنْتُ عَنْ
وُجودِ شُهُودِي مَاحِياً غَيْرَ مُثْبِتِ
وَعَانَقْتُ ما شَاهَدْتُ في مَحْوِ شاهِدِي
بِمَشْهَدِهِ لِلصَّحْوِ مِنْ بَعْدِ سَكْرَتِي
فَفِي الصَّحْوِ بَعْدَ المَحْوِ لَمْ أكُ غَيْرَها
وَذاتِي بِذَاتِي إِذْ تَحَلَّتْ تَجَلَّتِ
فَوَصْفِيَ إِذْ لَمْ تُدْعَ بِاثْنَيْنِ وَصْفُهَا
وَهَيْئَتُهَا إِذْ وَاحِدٌ نَحْنُ هَيئَتِي
فإِنْ دُعِيَتْ كُنْتُ المُجِيبَ وَإِنْ أكُنْ
مُنَادَى أجابَتْ مَنْ دَعَانِي ولَبَّتِ
وَإِنْ نَطَقَتْ كُنْتُ المُناجِي كَذاكَ إِنْ
قَصَصْتُ حَدِيثاً إِنَّمَا هِيَ قَصَّتِ
فَقَدْ رُفِعَتْ تَاءُ المُخَاطِبِ بَيْنَنَا
وَفي رَفْعِهَا عَنْ فُرْقَةِ الفَرْقِ رِفْعَتِي

٥٥

وَفَارِقْ ضَلالَ الفَرْقِ فَالجَمْعُ مُنْتِجٌ هُدَى فُرْقَةٍ بِالاتِّحادِ تَحَدَّتِ
وَصَرِّحْ بِإِطْلاقِ الجَمَالِ وَلا تَقُلْ بِتَقْيِيدِهِ مَيْلاً لِزُخْرُفِ زِينَةِ
فَكُلُّ مَلِيحٍ حُسْنُهُ مِنْ جَمَالِها مُعَارٌ لَهُ بَلْ حُسْنُ كُلِّ مَلِيحَةِ
بِها قَيْسُ لُبْنَى هَامَ بَلْ كُلُّ عاشِقٍ كَمَجْنُونِ لَيْلَى أَوْ كُثَيِّرِ عَزَّةِ

56

In every guise to yearning lovers She appeared,
Arrayed in forms most marvellous in their loveliness.
Thus on a time by name of Lubnā She is called,
And now Buthaynah, now again the longed-for ʿAzzah.[90]
Other than She they are not, no, nor ever were,
For in Her beauty She without a sharer is.
Even so, as She in others unto me appeared,
Clad in their forms, so I, united with Her beauty,
Appeared to Her in every lover thralled by love
Of youth or maid of wonder-striking loveliness.
Although before me, other than I these lovers were not,
Since them I had preceded in the Eternal Nights.
Other than I men are not in their love for Her,
I manifest myself in them in every guise.
I have been Qays, then as Kuthayyir I was seen,
Then yet again I was Jamīl who loved Buthaynah,
Outwardly manifest in them, yet veiled by them—
O marvel how I show a thing by hiding it!
Beyond delusion, they and they, women and men,
Theophanies are, where love and beauty We display.
Thus every loved one's man am I, She every man's
Belovèd, and each one a name is of disguise,

٥٦

وَتَظْهَرُ لِلعُشّاقِ في كُلِّ مَظْهَرٍ
مِنَ اللُّبْسِ في أَشْكالِ حُسْنٍ بَدِيعَةِ
فَفي مَرَّةٍ لُبْنَى وَأُخرَى بُثَيْنَةٌ
وَآوِنَةً تُدْعَى بِعَزَّةَ عَزَّتِ
وَلَسْنَ سِوَاهَا لاَ ولاَ كُنَّ غَيْرَها
وَمَا إِنْ لَها في حُسْنِها مِنْ شَرِيكَةِ
كَذاكَ بِحُكْمِ الاتِّحادِ بِحُسْنِها
كما قَدْ بَدَتْ في غَيْرِها وَتَزَيَّتِ
بَدَوْتُ لَها في كُلِّ صَبٍّ مُتَيَّمٍ
بِأَيِّ بَدِيعٍ حُسْنُهُ وَبِأَيَّةِ
وَلَيْسُوا بِغَيْرِي في الهَوَى لِتقَدُّمٍ
عَلَيَّ لِسَبْقٍ في اللَّيالِي القَدِيمَةِ
وَمَا القَوْمُ غَيْرِي في هَوَاهَا وَإِنّما
ظَهَرْتُ لَهُمْ لِلُّبْسِ في كُلِّ هَيْئَةِ
فَفي مَرَّةٍ قَيْساً وَأُخْرَى كُثَيِّراً
وَآوِنَةً أَبْدُو جَمِيلَ بُثَيْنَةِ
تَجَلَّيْتُ فِيهِم ظاهِراً واحتجَبْتُ بَا
طِناً بِهِمُ فأعْجَبْ لِكَشْفٍ بِسُتْرَةِ
وَهُنَّ وَهُمْ لا وَهْنَ وَهْمٍ مَظاهِرٌ
لنا بِتَجَلِّينا بِحُبٍّ وَنَضْرَةِ
فَكُلُّ فَتى حُبٍ أنا هُوَ وَهْيَ حُـ
ـبُّ كُلِّ فَتًى والْكُلُّ أَسْماءُ لُبْسَةِ

Names wherewith I the namèd was in very truth;
For I to Me appeared in them, with Self concealed.
I ever She am, and She I hath ever been—
No difference, but it was Myself that loved Myself,
And there is nothing with Me in the world but I,
No thoughts of with-ness trespass mine intelligence.[91]

أَسَامٍ بِهَا كُنْتُ المُسَمَّى حَقِيقَةً
وَكُنْتُ لِيَ البَادِي بِنَفْسٍ تَخَفَّتِ
وَمَا زِلْتُ إِيَّاهَا وَإِيَّايَ لَمْ تَزَلْ
وَلا فَرْقَ بَلْ ذَاتِي لِذَاتِي أَحَبَّتِ
وَلَيْسَ مَعِي فِي المُلْكِ شَيْءٌ سِوَاىَ وَالْ
مَعِيَّةُ لَمْ تَخْطُرْ على أَلْمَعِيَّةِ

13

Abū'l-Ḥasan ʿAlī ibn ʿAbd Allāh ash-Shushtarī of Andalusia

(d. 668 AH/1268-9 AD)

Shushtarī was a generation younger than the two poets who precede him here. Like Ibn ʿArabī, he was born in Muslim Spain and like him he went to Morocco where he must have spent enough time to be able to identify himself with the city of Meknes, since he speaks of himself in one of his lyrics as 'A shaykhling from the land of Meknes'. Again like Ibn ʿArabī, he went to the Near East, that is, to Egypt, Syria and Lebanon, with many pilgrimages to Mecca. It was Egypt that became as it were his home, and it was there that he died.

He took spiritual guidance from more than one of the most eminent Sufi Shaykhs of his day, but he must be considered as the disciple of Ibn Sabʿīn, a man some four years younger than himself who was also born in Andalusia, though their first meeting took place in Algeria when they were in their mid-thirties. Later they were together in Egypt and at Mecca. Both were men of learning and Shushtarī wrote one or two treatises on Sufism. He dedicated three poems to Ibn Sabʿīn, in one of which he calls him 'the magnet of souls', speaking of himself as 'his slave'. Ibn Sabʿīn seems to have appreciated and encouraged 'his slave's' gift for music. Shushtarī would often chant his lyrics when he was walking or riding, and he would sometimes accompany himself on a stringed instrument. In his last years he had many disciples, some of whom were very poor and, like himself, of a nomadic disposition.

Much of what he wrote in verse, especially what was not in classical Arabic,[92] cannot be called poetry in the strict sense; but verse can serve also the purpose, sometimes more effectively than prose, of conveying a significant truth to disciples and fixing it unforgettably in their intelligences; nor is Shushtarī the only Sufi who has taken advantage of this. He was nonetheless a truly gifted poet, as will be seen from the two examples of his art which are given here.

The first of these, as regards its content, recalls certain already quoted passages from Ibn al-Fāriḍ, but as the reader will see it is very different in style. Ibn ʿArabī is thought to have been the first to write in this particular form, the lyric in stanzas with a change of rhyme (*ghazal*). The translation given here maintains a rhythm close to that of the original. But Shushtarī also wrote poems in the traditional metres of Arabic poetry, and one of these is the second of the two poems given here. It is said to have been written in Libya after he had been called a madman for rejecting the post of *Qāḍī* [93] which the authorities of Tripoli had offered him.

57

Truly I am a wondrous thing
For him who sees me:
Lover and Beloved, both am I,
There is no second.
O seeker of the essential Truth,
Thine eye's film hides it.
Return unto thyself, take note:
None is but thee.
All good, all knowledge springs from thee;
In thee's the Secret.
Thou the mirror[94] art for gazing,
Pole of the times.
Stored up in thee is what's poured forth
from all the vessels.
Hear my word and drink it in,
If thou canst grasp it:
Thy treasure naked is, not hid
'Neath riddling spell.
There Speaker, Spoken-to are on[95]
The mount of knowledge.
Hearken to my call from near,
Not with thine ears.
My self's sun setteth ne'er from vision
Face to face.
Behold My beauty, witness of Me
In every man,
Like the water flowing through
The sap of branches.
One water drink they, yet they flower
In many hues.
In awe of Majesty prostrate thee
As thou approachest.
Perfection's verses, oft repeated,
Recite, the seven.[96]

٥٧

أَنـا شَيءٌ عَـجـيـبٌ لِـمَـنْ رَآنِي
أَنـا المُحِـبُّ والحَـبِـيـبُ لَيْس ثَمَّ ثانِي
يـا قـاصِـدًا عَيْنَ الخَـبَرْ غـطَّـتْهُ عَيْنُكَ
ارْجَـعْ لِـذَاتِـكَ واعْـتـبِرْ مَـا ثَمَّ غَـيْرُكَا
فـالخَـيْرُ مِـنْـك والخَـبَرْ والـسِّرُّ عِـنْـدَكَ
وأنْـت مِـرْآةُ الـنَّـظَـرْ قُـطْـبُ الزَّمَـانِ
وَفِـيكَ يُطْـوَى ما انْـتَـشَرْ مِـنَ الأَوَانِي
اسْمَـعْ كَلاَمِي والْـتَهِـمْ إِنْ كُنْت تَفْهَامِ
لأَنَّ كَـنْزَكَ قَـدْ عَـرَى عَنْ كُلِّ طَلْسَامِ
مِـنْـهُ المُـكَلَّـمُ والـكَلِيمُ عَلَى طُورِ الأَفُهَامِ
اسْمَعْ نِـدَايَ مِنْ قـرِيـبْ بِـــلاَ أَذَانِ
وَشَمْـسُ ذَاتِي لا تَـغِـيـبْ عَـنِ الْـعَـيَـانِ
انْـظُـرْ جَمَـالِي شَـاهِـداً فِي كُلِّ إِنْـسَانِ
كالمَـاءِ يَجْـرِى نـافِـذاً فِي أُسِ الأَغْـصَانِ
يُـسْـقَـى بِمَـاءٍ واحِـدٍ والـزَّهْـرُ أَلْـوَانِ
فاسْجُدْ لِهَيْبَةِ ذِي الجَلالِ عِـنْـدَ الـتَّـدَانِي
وَلِـتَـقْـرَأَ آيـاتِ الـكَـمـالِ سَـبْـعـاً مَـثَـانِي

58

After extinction I came out, and I
Eternal now am, though not as I.
And who am I, O I, but I.[97]

59

The slave to love well pleased is with his madness.
Let him wear out his life even as he will.
Reprove him not; your blame will nothing serve:
Forsaking love is not in his religion.
I swear by him for whom ʿAqīq was mentioned—[98]
A lover's oath by his belovèd—none
But ye are mine; yet have I to repent me[99]
Remissnesses in loving, waveringness.
Why, when I hear the dove coo in the glade,
Why yearn I ever at his sorrowing?
And though his way is weeping without tears,
When lover weeps, the tears pour from his eyes.[100]

٥٨

خَرَجْتُ في حِينٍ بَعْدَ الفَنَا
وَمِنْ هُنَا بَقِيتُ بِلاَ أَنَا
وَمِنْ أَنَا يا أَنَا إلاَّ أَنَا

٥٩

رَضِيَ المُتَيَّمُ في الهَوىَ بجُنونِهِ
خَلُّوهُ يَفنَى عُمْرَه بِفُنونِهِ
لاتعْذِلوهُ فَلَيْسَ يَنْفعُ عَذْلُكُمْ
لَيْسَ السُلُوُّ عَنِ الْهَوى مِنْ دِينِهِ
قَسَمًا بِمَنْ ذِكِرَ العَقِيقُ مِنْ أَجْلِهِ
قَسَمَ المُحِبُّ بِحُبِّهِ وَيَمِينِهِ
مَالي سِواكُمْ غَيْرَ أَنّي تَائِبٌ
عَنْ فَاتِرَاتِ الحُبِّ أَوْ تَلْوِينِهِ
مَالي إذا هَتَفَ الحَمَامُ بِأَيْكَةٍ
أَبَداً أَحِنُّ لِشَجْوِهِ وشُجُونِهِ
وإذا البُكاءُ بِغَيْرِ دَمْعٍ دَأْبُهُ
والصَّبُ يَجْرِي دَمْعُهُ بِعُيُونِهِ

Conclusion

In concluding this brief collection, let us add some lines which were not in origin a Sufi poem, but which have nonetheless been as it were annexed into Sufism. In fact they were addressed to Sayf ad-Dawlah, a prince of the Ḥamdānid family, by his younger cousin, the gifted poet Abū Firās al-Ḥamdānī who died in 968 AD. The lines themselves have an undeniable beauty, in virtue of which they would inevitably be quoted sometimes out of context; and hearing them thus, any spiritual man would immediately assume that they were addressed to God, and that they must have been composed by one of the Sufi poets. Some have attributed them to Ḥallāj;[101] others have looked elsewhere, but in any case they have long been known and loved as one of the great poetic treasures of Sufism. The Sufi Shaykh Mūlāy al-ʿArabī ad-Darqāwī tells us that his Shaykh, Mūlāy ʿAlī al-Jamal, if asked what was his favourite poem, would answer by reciting these lines:

60

So Thou be sweet, let life run bitterly;
So Thou be pleased, let men be wroth with me;
So all things flourish between me and Thee,
Let all between me and the world in ruins be.[102]

وَلَيْتَكَ تَحْلُو والحَياةُ مَرِيرةٌ وَلَيْتَك تَرْضَى وَالأَنَامُ غِضَابُ
وَلَيْتَ الّذِي بيْني وَبَيْنِكَ عَامِرٌ وبَيْنِي وَبَيْنَ العالَمِينَ خَرَابُ

Not far in meaning from these lines are two much loved anonymous lines of Sufi poetry which have been faithfully handed down throughout the centuries; and with these we will finally end this collection:

61

The soul is precious, yet for Thee will I exchange her;
And being slain is bitter, but in Thy good pleasure it is sweet.

النَّفْسُ عَزَّتْ ولَكِنْ فِيكَ أَبْذُلُها وَالْقَتْلُ مُرٌّ وَلَكِنْ في رِضاكَ حَلا

Notes

[1]Martin Lings, *What is Sufism?*, Cambridge, The Islamic Texts Society, 1993, p. 106.

[2]*Ibid.*, pp. 97–8.

[3]Abū Ṭālib al-Makkī, *Qūt al-qulūb*, 2 vols., Cairo, 1310/1893, II, p. 57; ʿAbd ar-Raḥmān Badawī, *Shahīdat al-ʿishq al-ilāhī Rābiʿah al-ʿAdawiyyah*, Cairo, Maktabat an-Nahḍa al-Miṣriyyah, 1962 (second edition), p. 110.

[4]Badawī, p. 52.

[5]These lines, which she is said to have heard recited to her in her sleep, may be considered as hers by inspiration. Badawī, p. 134.

[6]From the basic Arabic root *khā'–lām–lām* are derived the words *takhallul* (intimate penetration) and *khalīl* (intimate friend).

[7]Badawī, pp. 61 and 120.

[8]ʿAbd ar-Raḥmān as-Sulamī, *Ṭabaqāt aṣ-ṣūfiyyah*, ed. N. Sharība, Cairo, Dār al-Kitāb al-ʿArabī, 1953, pp. 28–9; also edited by J. Pedersen as *Kitāb ṭabaqāt aṣ-ṣūfiyya*, Leiden, Brill, 1960, p. 21; Abū Naṣr as-Sarrāj, *The Kitāb al-Lumaʿ fī 't-taṣawwuf*, ed. R. A. Nicholson, Gibb Memorial Series, no. 22, Leiden and London, 1914, p. 368.

[9]Abū Nuʿaym al-Iṣfahānī, *Ḥilyat al-awliyā'*, 10 vols., Cairo, Maktabat as-Saʿāda, 1932–38, IX, p. 369 and p. 391 (variants).

[10]Cf. Qur'ān, LXXXII, 11–12.

[11]*Shawāhid* (witnesses, proofs): each particular example of knowledge derived from the sciences is not only an eloquent sign that the knower in question is a true gnostic, but also a criterion for judging false claims to gnosis.

[12]Iṣfahānī (*Ḥilyat al-awliyā'*, X, p. 200) seems to attribute the poem to Sahl, but gives only the first line. Sahl may however have been quoting from an earlier poet (see Nīsābūrī, *ʿUqalā' al- majānīn*, ed. W. F. al-Kīlānī, Cairo, 1924, pp. 129–30). The above translation is from the recension given

by Massignon, who considers the poem to be by Sahl (see Massignon, *Le Dīwān d'al-Ḥallāj*, Paris, Paul Geuthner, 1955, p. 115).

[13]This must not be taken, here or elsewhere, to mean that the Sufi in question wrote no poems.

[14]*Zanjī*, which can also mean negro.

[15]In Sufism 'Nearness' signifies Identity in virtue of the Divine affirmation: *We are nearer to him [man] than his jugular vein* (Qur'ān, L, 16).

[16]Abū Bakr Muḥammad al-Kalābādhī, *Kitāb at-taʿarruf li-madhhab ahl at-taṣawwuf*, ed. A. Ḥ. Maḥmūd and Ṭ. A. B. Surūr, Cairo, 1960, ch. 46. (see also Arberry's translation, *The Doctrine of the Sufis*, Cambridge, Cambridge University Press, 1935, p. 97).

[17]Abū'l-Qāsim al-Qushayrī, *Risālat al-Qushayrī*, ed. A. Ḥ. Maḥmud and M. ash-Sharīf, Cairo, Dār al-Kitāb al-Ḥadīth, 1966, p. 199.

[18]Massignon, *Le Dīwān d'al-Ḥallāj*, p. 118.

[19]Kalābādhī, ch. 56.

[20]*Ibid.*, ch. 47.

[21]Sarrāj, *Kitāb al-Lumaʿ*, p. 250. The poem as a whole is too abstruse to fit into the context of this book.

[22]Sulamī, *Ṭabaqāt* (ed. Sharība), p. 197; see also Pedersen's edition, p. 188. It is difficult to convey in English the effect of the final cry *wā ʿaṭashī* ('Oh, my thirst!').

[23]Louis Massignon, *Recueil des textes inédits concernant l'histoire de la mystique en pays d'Islam*, Paris, Paul Geuthner, 1929, p. 72; Massignon, *Le Dīwān d'al-Ḥallāj*, p. 117.

[24]Sulamī, *Ṭabaqāt*, ed. Sharība, p. 198; Pedersen's edition, p. 189.

[25]Sulamī, *Ṭabaqāt*, ed. Sharība, p. 198; Pedersen's edition, p. 191; Iṣfahānī, *Ḥilyat al-awliyā'*, X, p. 311; Ibn az-Zayyāt, *Tashawwuf ilā rijāl at-taṣawwuf*, ed. A. Faure, Rabat, Editions Techniques Nord-Africaines, 1958, p. 110 (anonymously).

[26]The mention of this large category of scholars obliges us to insist immediately that Louis Massignon cannot be said to belong to it. He was himself a truly spiritual man, and the more sensitive of his academic pupils in Paris were conscious, in his presence, of what might be termed a certain mystical radiance. One of them, the late and now well-known ʿUthmān Yaḥyā, a Muslim of Syrian origin who had settled in France, told me that he had felt so drawn towards his teacher that he had almost decided to become a Christian. But Massignon dissuaded him: 'You will find nothing,' he said, 'in Christianity that you cannot find in Sufism.' My brief exchange

of letters with ʿUthmān Yaḥyā took place in the early seventies before my retirement from work in the British Library. It seemed to me that he evinced an unquestioning acceptance of all that Massignon wrote about Sufism, including the erroneous opinion that the doctrine of *Waḥdat al-Wujūd* (Oneness of Being) had been introduced into Sufism by Muḥyi'd-Dīn Ibn ʿArabī who was thus responsible for what the French scholar saw as a rapid falling away from the true Sufism of Ḥallāj. In my reply I pointed out that the doctrine of *Waḥdat al-Wujūd* comes from the Qur'ān itself and that Ḥallāj's spiritual life was based on it as were the lives of his great Sufi contemporaries and predecessors, no less that the lives of Ibn ʿArabī and his followers; and I gave him the reference to chapter 5, 'Oneness of Being', in my book *A Sufi Saint of the Twentieth Century.* I was also critical of Massignon's underestimation of Ibn ʿArabī. My letter produced no answering letter, and I continued to draw wrong conclusions from this silence until, some years later, I learned that ʿUthmān Yaḥyā had in fact answered my letter in a very positive way by becoming something of a devotee of Ibn ʿArabī, with much time spent on the search for manuscripts of his many apparently lost works throughout a large number of libraries in the East and West, some of them private collections as yet uncatalogued. He is perhaps best known for his book *Histoire et Classification de l'Œuvre d'Ibn ʿArabī.*

As to Massignon, despite his misunderstanding of the doctrine of Oneness of Being, an error which he shares with Nicholson, Gairdner and others of his orientalist contemporaries, we must nonetheless be grateful to him for having been so intensely aware of the spiritual greatness of Ḥallāj. His book, *Le Dīwān d'al-Ḥallāj*, should never have been allowed to go out of print.

[27]Massignon, *Le Dīwān d'al-Ḥallāj*, p. 86.

[28]*Ibid.*, p. 75.

[29]*Ibid.*, p. 90.

[30]*Ibid.*, p. 46.

[31]*Ibid.*, p. 103.

[32]*Ibid.*, p. 58.

[33]*Ibid.*, pp. 38–9.

[34]*Ibid.*, p. 67.

[35]*Ibid.*, p. 59.

[36]*Ibid.*, p. 42.

[37]*Ibid.*, p. 85. When pilgrims arrive in Mecca the first rite they perform is to visit the Kaʿbah and to walk round it seven times.

[38] *Ibid.*, p. 84.

[39] *Ibid.*, p. 66.

[40] *Ibid.*, p. 37.

[41] *Ibid.*, p. 61.

[42] *Ibid.*, p. 71.

[43] In other words, the Mystery referred to precedes all creation, since according to the Prophet the Pen, then the Tablet, were the first two things to be created. *Ibid.*, p. 88.

[44] *Ibid.*, p. 93.

[45] *Ibid.*, p. 77.

[46] Abū Bakr ash-Shiblī, *Dīwān*, ed. K. M. al-Shaybī, Baghdad, Dār al-Taḍāmun, 1967, p. 119.

[47] When the object of love is plural in Sufi poetry, the reference is to the Divine Qualities.

[48] Shiblī, *Dīwān*, p. 112.

[49] 'For the eager to despair': throughout the Qur'ān, the rain-cloud stands for the promise of divine bounty (panegyric poetry, *madīḥ*, uses the same image for the patron's munificence). Sarrāj, *Kitāb al-Lumaʿ*, p. 251 and p. 403; Shiblī, *Dīwān*, p. 142.

[50] Sarrāj, *Kitāb al-Lumaʿ*, pp. 252–253.

[51] The divinity is frequently referred to in Sufi poetry by a woman's name, most often Laylā, the beloved of Majnūn, or by the feminine pronoun.

[52] Shiblī, *Dīwān*, p. 170; Iṣfahānī, *Ḥilyat al-awliyā'*, X, p. 373.

[53] Shiblī, *Dīwān*, p. 88.

[54] Ibn az-Zayyāt, *Tashawwuf*, p. 108 (anonymously); Sarrāj, *Kitāb al-Lumaʿ*, p. 365.

[55] Iṣfahānī, *Ḥilyat al-awliyā'*, X, p. 372.

[56] Sulamī, *Ṭabaqāt*, ed. Sharība, p. 444; Pedersen's edition, pp. 464–5; Ibn az-Zayyāt, *Tashawwuf*, p. 242 (less complete and unattributed).

[57] Ibn az-Zayyāt, *Tashawwuf*, p. 69; the 'best of deeds' is invocation of the name of God (*dhikr Allāh*). The word *dhikr* is a synthesis of the English words 'remembrance' and 'mention'. The Qur'ān affirms the altogether superlative nature of *dhikr Allāh* (Q. XXIX: 45), and it is the very basis of Sufi practice.

[58]Brit. Mus. Add. 76561; M. al-Murtaḍā, *Itḥāf as-Sādah*, Cairo, 1311 AH, p. 43. There is a full translation in Margaret Smith, *Al-Ghazālī the Mystic* (London, Luzac & Co., 1944, p. 36), evidently from a different recension. Although the poem is also attributed to others, in particular to Abū Ḥāmid's brother, Aḥmad al-Ghazālī (d. 520 AH/1126 AD), and to Abū'l-Ḥasan ʿAlī as-Sibṭī (d. 600 AH/1203 AD), Pedersen remarks that the weight of manuscript authority is strongly in favour of the attribution to Abū Ḥāmid ('Ein Gedicht al-Gazālīs', *Le Monde Oriental*, 1931, XXV).

[59]As we have already seen (note 47), when the object of love is plural in Sufi poetry, the reference is to the Divine Qualities.

[60]In telling us, as his commentary does, that his question was addressed to those who had helped him in the past on his spiritual path, he speaks as one who is accustomed to communicate with the dead. Their answer, that the riders rest under the *shīḥ* and *bān* trees, whose fragrances stand respectively for yearning inclination towards the loved ones and sad consciousness of their remoteness, may be taken as an injunction to increase his own yearning and his own sense of being abandoned, in other words, to draw them back to him by his own increased spiritual fragrance.

[61]Ibn ʿArabī, *The Tarjumān al-Ashwāq: A Collection of Mystical Odes by Muḥyī'ddīn ibn al-ʿArabī*, ed. and trans. by R. A. Nicholson, London, Theosophical Publishing House, 1911, VI, p. 17.

[62]I.e. as each new moon does in relation to the old moon.

[63]Ibn ʿArabī, *Tarjumān*, XL, p. 36.

[64]*Ibid.*, XI, p. 19. Qays (Majnūn, 'Madman') and Laylā are the only pair of these lovers who can be considered as world-famous. One of the manuscripts reads, instead of Laylā, Lubnā whose Qays is a different man from Qays al-Majnūn, and Nicholson has preferred the reading 'Lubnā' for his translation.

[65]With the infinite reality of God, of which water is the symbol; so also in the final line of the poem. See Martin Lings, *Symbol & Archetype*, Cambridge, Quinta Essentia, 1991, chapter 7: 'The Qur'ānic Symbolism of Water'.

[66]The ritual ablution must be performed with sand, etc., in the absence of water; the allusion in this is to those who have not achieved gnosis. The following line could be paraphrased: 'But the gnostic has the right to remain in the background and to keep secret his Secret.'

[67]Combine illumination (or escape from darkness, i.e. dawn) with readiness to receive it, spiritual maturity (mid-afternoon).

[68]See Shaʿrānī, *at-Ṭabaqāt al-kubrā*, 2 vols., Cairo, 1343/1925, II p. 63 (s. v. Muḥammad Abū'l-Mawāhib ash-Shādhilī, who quotes and interprets the lines); see also Abū'l-Mawāhib ash-Shādhilī, *Qawānīn ḥikam al-ishrāq*,

ed. and trans. E. J. Jurji as *Illumination in Islamic Mysticism*, Princeton, Princeton University Press, 1938, pp. 80–1.

[69]The poet is here referring to what he names elsewhere *al-Aʿyān ath-thābitah* (the Immutable Archetypes), that is, our pre-creational realities in the Hidden Treasure of the Divine Substance. Very relevant to this poem is what Sufis and many others believe to be a 'Holy Tradition' of the Prophet, Holy because it is not he but God Himself who is speaking on his tongue: 'I was a Hidden Treasure and I loved to be known and so I created the world.' Each of the 'letters not yet uttered' may be likened to an as yet unseen precious jewel in the Hidden Treasure Itself though it must be born in mind that at this transcendent level the part mysteriously partakes of the whole. It is from these archetypes that we originate, and it is to them that we seek to return as the last line of the poem implies. The pronoun 'Thou' signifies the Personal God, God the Creator, Who is nonetheless inseparable from the Absolute Infinite Eternal Perfection of His Own Essence, which is 'He'. There is a Sufi saying: '*Ash-Sharīʿah* (the religion as such, binding on everyone): I am I and Thou art Thou; *aṭ-Ṭarīqah* (the path of the Sufis): I am Thou and Thou art I; *al-Ḥaqīqah* (the Truth, the Reality): No I, no Thou: He.' See ʿAbd ar-Razzāq al-Qāshānī, *Laṭā'if al-aghlām fī ishārāt ahl al-ilhām: muʿjam al-muṣṭalaḥāt wa'l-ishārāt aṣ-ṣūfiyya*, ed. Saʿīd ʿAbd al-Fattāḥ, Cairo, Dār al-Kutub al-Miṣriyya, 1995, vol. 1, p. 407.

[70]This poem, here translated into blank verse, was translated into prose by Nicholson in his *Studies in Islamic Mysticism*, Cambridge, Cambridge University Press, 1921, pp. 184–88, and by Arberry in *The Mystical Poems of Ibn al-Fārid* (Chester Beatty Monographs 4, London, Emery Walker, 1952), pp. 81–84. For the Arabic, see Arberry *ibid.*, pp. 39–41, edited in transcription from the oldest manuscript, and *Dīwān Ibn al-Fāriḍ*, an undated Cairo edition probably from the first half of the twentieth century, annotated and published by Maḥmūd Tawfīq, pp. 82–84.

[71]The reference is to the *dhikr*, the remembrance or invocation of the Name of God, the basic rite of Islamic mysticism. It is to this Name that every mention of the wine's name refers throughout the poem. The tribe is the brotherhood.

[72]The Prophet is not only the cup, but also, as Seal of the Prophets, the seal upon the wine-jar.

[73]Literally 'unveil her', for *khamr* (wine) is feminine. As Arberry remarks in the notes to his translation, the comparison of the unveiling of the becobwebbed wine-jar with the unveiling of a bride is frequent 'in bacchic poetry'.

[74]The riders are the advanced initiates, *sālikūn* (travellers), who are immune from the effects of poison which, according to ʿAbd al-Ghanī Nābulusī—who wrote a commentary on the *Dīwān* of Ibn al-Fāriḍ—is the passionate attachment to worldly things. (Cf. an-Nābulusī, *Sharḥ dīwān Ibn al-Fāriḍ*, 2 vols., Cairo, al-Maṭbaʿah al-Azhariyyah, 1319AH

[75]Again according to Nābulusī, the enchanter is the Spiritual Master and the madman is one who takes appearances for reality.

[76]Another reference to the brotherhood, this time as an army whose warriors are engaged in the Greater Holy War (*al-jihād al-akbar*), 'the war against the soul'.

[77]Every human being is in love with the wine even if he be not conscious of it. The descriptions of it serve to awaken that latent love. Nuʿm, like Laylā, is one of those women's names by which Sufis denote the Divine Essence. Love of Nuʿm and love of the wine may therefore be said to coincide.

[78]At the level of my oneness with the principial wine in Eternity—wine which, being absolutely independent, is therefore in no need of grape or vine for its existence—I am a true son of Adam who, as Logos, prefigures my union by his. The vine is *Nafas ar-Raḥmān* (the Breath of the All-Merciful) which is also termed *aṭ-Ṭabīʿah* (Universal Nature), the feminine or maternal source of all manifestation.

[79]Reading *tasmū* as in the oldest manuscript. It is for the mystic to ensure, by the ritual means at his disposal, that his soul is filled with spiritual presences or truths. These presences have a purifying effect upon the soul, which is their vessel, and this increase of purity qualifies the vessel to endure a heightening of the truths. If we read *tanmū*, 'have increase', as in the other manuscripts, the meaning is not basically changed.

[80]But, as Nābulusī remarks, the vine contains the spiritual juice which will ultimately be transmuted into wine. We may compare the lines of Ibn al-Fāriḍ's younger contemporary, ʿAlī ash-Shushtarī:

> Behold My beauty, witness of Me
> In every man,
> Like the water flowing through
> The sap of branches.
> One water drink they, yet they flower
> In many hues.

[81]It is not the spiritual or 'winal' nature of Adam which is referred to here but his human or 'vineal' nature, of which the Prophet said: 'I was a Prophet when Adam was yet between water and clay', while nonetheless having to speak of his own spiritual nature in answer to the question 'When did you become a Prophet?'

[82]If you have not the spiritual strength for oneness with the Divine Essence Itself, then let the water that you mix the wine with be nothing less than 'the saliva of God', that is, the Supreme Spirit, which, if it be not fully Him, is not other than Him. The mixing of the wine thus signifies the emergence of the Logos, *ar-Rūḥ al-Muḥammadī*, and this explains the mention of stars in line 4. The manifestation of the Spirit of Muḥammad precipitates the existence of the Spirits of his Companions, whom he likened

to stars: 'My companions are even as the stars. Whichsoever of them ye follow, ye shall be rightly guided.' By extension the words 'how many stars' may be taken to include those Saints who are heirs of the Companions in subsequent generations.

[83]God's reply to Moses when he asked the same favour, Qur'ān, VII, 143–4; see note 95.

[84]Ibn al-Fāriḍ, *Dīwān Ibn al-Fāriḍ*, p. 99.

[85]Although Muḥammad is after Jacob in time, his spirit is the starting-point of creation and therefore needs to be 'remembered' by Jacob.

[86]Ibn al-Fāriḍ, *Dīwān Ibn al-Fāriḍ*, p. 99; Arberry, *ibid.*, p. 30, lines 38–42.

[87]Ibn al-Fāriḍ, *Dīwān Ibn al-Fāriḍ*, pp. 35–36; Arberry, *ibid.*, p. 78, lines 214–8.

[88]See note 64.

[89]Arberry, *ibid.*, p. 80, lines 240–243.

[90]Buthaynah was the beloved of Jamīl, and ʿAzzah of Kuthayyir.

[91]Ibn al-Fāriḍ, *Dīwān Ibn al-Fāriḍ*, pp. 37–38; Arberry, *ibid.*, pp. 80–81, lines 251–264; .

[92]Shushtarī is perhaps the first Sufi poet to have made use of the vernacular in this way.

[93]Judge.

[94]Primordial man, that is, man as he was created in the image of God may be said to mirror God. A supreme Saint is thus the mirror of mirrors to be gazed into in order to see what God wishes His representative on earth to be. If it be objected that one looks into a mirror to see oneself, the answer is that here lies the highest meaning of Shushtarī's line. The ultimate aim and end of Sufism and of its equivalent in other religions is to realise one's True Self, the One and Only Divine Self, or in other words to attain to the degree of the Supreme Identity.

[95]*Al-Kalīm*: Moses, in the Qur'ān the forerunner of Muḥammad and the only mortal to whom God has spoken '*except by inspiration or from behind a veil*' (Qur'ān, XLII, 50–1) or through an angelic intermediary: '*He said, O Lord, shew me thy glory, that I may behold thee. God answered, Thou shalt in no wise behold me; but look towards the mountain, and if it stands firm in its place, then shalt thou see me. But when his Lord appeared in glory in the mount, He reduced it to dust... God said unto him, O Moses, I have chosen thee above all men... by speaking unto thee.*' Qur'ān, VII, 143–4, (trans. Sale, *The Korân*).

[96]I.e. *Sūrat al-Fātiḥah*, the first chapter of the Qur'ān; it has seven verses. Shushtarī, *Dīwān*, ed. A. S. an-Nashshār, Alexandria, Dār al-Maʿārif, 1960, p. 267.

[97]This poem does not appear in Shushtarī's *Dīwān*. However, the Shaykh al-ʿAlawī quoted it more than once and attributed it to Shushtarī. See *A Sufi Saint of the Twentieth Century*, p. 127.

[98]A valley near Medina through which the route to Mecca passes. An angel told the Prophet that ʿAqīq was especially blessed by God.

[99]Fallen man is by definition fragmented and chaotic. Sufism is the Islamic means of reawakening everything in the soul that has become dormant and of restoring each psychic element to its right place. One of the dangers of the spiritual path is that the modest early stages of spiritual progress should be mistaken for the finality, and that the soul in question should suppose that the end had been reached. This is one of the reasons for the insistence, by so many of the Sufi Shaykhs, on the use of the third personal pronoun to express the Supreme Reality. We have already seen a striking example of this insistence at the end of poem 50. As to the second personal pronoun, it affirms a duality which appears to contradict the doctrine of Absolute Oneness. With regard to the beautifully emphatic use of the second person in the opening *Sūrah* of the Qur'ān which forms the basis of the Islamic ritual prayer, *Thee we worship and from Thee we seek help*, Sufis have been known to say that if the Prophet himself had not recited these words they themselves would be unwilling to do so.

As to Shushtarī's brief poem, the second line seems to be a dutiful acceptance of the use of the third person, but the third line gives us a sudden and unexpected protest from the first person. It was no doubt this line which endeared the poem to the Shaykh al-ʿAlawī who quotes it more than once. He himself, in his aphorisms, affirms the inadequacy of all three of the personal pronouns including the third which is blamed for its lack of any inclusive element. (See *A Sufi Saint of the Twentieth Century*, p. 206.)

[100]Shushtarī, *Dīwān*, p. 77.

[101]See Massignon, *Le Dīwān d'al-Ḥallāj*, p. 119.

[102]Abū Firās al-Ḥamdānī, *Dīwān*, Beirut, Dār Ṣādir, 1959, p. 27.

Bibliography

Arberry, A. J., *The Doctrine of the Sufis*, Cambridge, Cambridge University Press, 1935.

——— *The Mystical Poems of Ibn al-Fāriḍ*, Chester Beatty Monograph 4, London, Emery Walker, 1952.

——— *The Mystical Poems of Ibn al-Fāriḍ*, Dublin, 1956.

Ashtiany, J. (ed.), *ʿAbbasid Belles-Lettres*, Cambridge, Cambridge University Press, 1990.

al-Badawī, ʿAbd ar-Raḥmān, *Shāhidat al-ʿishq al-ilāhī Rābiʿah al-ʿAdawiyyah*, 2nd ed., Cairo, Maktabat an-Nahḍa al-Miṣriyyah, 1962.

al-Ḥallāj, Manṣūr, see Massignon.

al-Ḥamdānī, Abū Firās, *Dīwān*, Beirut, Dār Ṣādir, 1959.

Ibn ʿArabī, *The Tarjumān al-Ashwāq: a Collection of Mystical Odes by Muḥyī'ddīn ibn al-ʿArabī*, ed. and trans. by R. A. Nicholson, London, Theosophical Publishing House, 1911.

Ibn al-Fāriḍ, *Dīwān Ibn al-Fāriḍ*, ed. M. Tawfīq, Cairo, n.d.

Ibn az-Zayyāt, *at-Tashawwuf ilā rijāl at-taṣawwuf*, ed. A. Faure, Rabat, Editions Techniques Nord-Africaines, 1958.

al-Iṣfahānī, Abū Nuʿaym, *Ḥilyat al-awliyā'*, 10 volumes, Cairo, Maktabat as-Saʿāda, 1932–38.

al-Kalābādhī, *Kitāb at-taʿarruf li-madhhab ahl at-taṣawwuf*, edited by A. Ḥ. Maḥmūd and Ṭ. A. B. Surūr, Cairo, 1960; also trans.

by A. J. Arberry as *The Doctrine of the Sufis*, Cambridge, Cambridge University Press, 1935.

Lings, Martin, *A Sufi Saint of the Twentieth Century: Shaikh Aḥmad al-ʿAlawī, his Spiritual Heritage and Legacy*, Cambridge, Islamic Texts Society, 1993.

——— *Symbol & Archetype*, Cambridge, Quinta Essentia, 1991.

——— *What is Sufism?*, Cambridge, Islamic Texts Society, 1993.

al-Makkī, Abū Ṭālib, *Qūt al-qulūb*, 2 vols., Cairo, 1310/1893.

Massignon, Louis, *Le Dīwān d'al-Ḥallāj*, Paris, Paul Geuthner, 1955.

——— *Recueil de textes inédits concernant l'histoire de la mystique en pays d'Islam*, Paris, Paul Geuthner, 1929.

al-Murtaḍā, M., *Itḥāf as-Sādah*, Cairo, 1311 AH.

an-Nābulusī, ʿAbd al-Ghanī ibn Ismāʿīl, *Sharḥ dīwān Ibn al-Fāriḍ*, 2 vols., Cairo, al-Maṭbaʿah al-Azhariyyah, 1319AH.

Nicholson, R. A., *Studies in Islamic Mysticism*, Cambridge, Cambridge University Press, 1921.

an-Nīsābūrī, *ʿUqalāʾ al-majānīn*, ed. W. F. al-Kīlānī, Cairo, 1924.

Pedersen, J. (ed.), 'Ein Gedicht al-Gazālīs', *Le Monde Oriental*, XXV, 1931.

al-Qāshānī, ʿAbd ar-Razzāq, *Laṭāʾif al-aghlām fī ishārāt ahl al-ilhām: muʿjam al-muṣṭalaḥāt wa'l-ishārāt aṣ-ṣūfiyya*, edited by Saʿīd ʿAbd al-Fattāḥ, Cairo, Dār al-Kutub al-Miṣriyya, 1995.

al-Qushayrī, *Risālat al-Qushayrī*, ed. A. Ḥ. Maḥmūd and M. ash-Sharīf, Cairo, Dār al-Kitāb al-Ḥadīth, 1966.

Sale, George (trans.), *The Korân*, London, 1734.

as-Sarrāj, Abū Naṣr, *The Kitāb al-Lumaʿ fī 't-taṣawwuf*, edited by R. A. Nicholson, Gibb Memorial Series, no. 22, Leiden and London, 1914.

ash-Shādhilī, Abu'l-Mawāhib, *Qawānīn ḥikam al-ishrāq*, ed. and trans. E. J. Jurji as *Illuminations in Islamic Mysticism*, Princeton, Princeton University Press, 1938.

ash-Shaʿrānī, *aṭ-Ṭabaqāt al-kubrā*, 2 vols., Cairo, 1343/1925.

ash-Shiblī, *Dīwān*, ed. K. M. ash-Shaybī, Baghdad, Dār at-Taḍāmun, 1967.

ash-Shushtarī, *Dīwān*, ed. A. S. an-Nashshār, Alexandria, Dār al-Maʿārif, 1960.

Sirāj ad-Dīn, Abū Bakr, *The Book of Certainty*, Cambridge, Islamic Texts Society, 1992.

Smith, Margaret, *Al-Ghazālī the Mystic*, London, Luzac & Co., 1944.

as-Sulamī, *Ṭabaqāt aṣ-ṣufiyyah*, edited by N. Sharība, Cairo, Dār al-Kitāb al-ʿArabī, 1953; also edited by J. Pedersen, *Kitāb ṭabaqāt aṣ-ṣufiyya*, Leiden, Brill, 1960.

Yahia, Osman, *Histoire et Classification de l'Œuvre d'Ibn ʿArabī*, 2 volumes, Damascus, Institut Français de Damas, 1964.